LIFE AFTER MPD

A transcendental text for patient, professional, or
loved one for treating and understanding Dissociative
Identity Disorder or Multiple Personality Disorder.

Preface by
Christopher H. Rosik, Ph.D.

Foreword by
Geraldine H. Ferry, M.S., M.A., L.M.F.T., L.P.C.

Debra Lighthart Ph.D.

PO Box 221974 Anchorage, Alaska 99522-1974

ISBN 1-888125-76-4

Library of Congress Catalog Card Number: 00-108759

Copyright 2000 by Debra Lighthart Ph.D.
—First Edition—

Manufactured in the United States of America.

Dedication

This book is dedicated to individuals living with Multiple Personality Disorder and Post-Traumatic Stress Disorder, their families and friends who love them and watch them and the families and friends who suffer with them. You are not alone.

This book is dedicated to the pastors and therapists compassionately working with individuals diagnosed and families of those diagnosed with Multiple Personality Disorder and Post-Traumatic Stress Disorder. Take courage.

This book is dedicated to all those looking for healing of Multiple Personality Disorder and Post-Traumatic Stress Disorder. You are brave.

To all of these people, You are not alone. You are brave, and I hope you find the hope, encouragement, support, and strength I extend to you from the pages of this book.

Contents

Acknowledgments

To David and Lee I say thank you for your openness and willingness to recognize and utilize the resources I possessed within me that may or may not have fallen within the realm of your method or style of counseling. Your acceptance of my needs, and use of my strengths as an individual, brought a level of healing I needed, from not only the trauma I survived, but also brought healing to previous counseling experiences. You encouraged me to be true to myself then, and I remain so now.

I thank Susan Ohrberg who's editing and proofing of my manuscript made it ready to submit to a publisher.

I thank my husband and children for their support in the most difficult of situations. Your gift of time, loyalty, and patience helped me move through the pain.

I thank my parents for teaching me persistence, perseverance and a work ethic of not giving up. Without those gifts I would not have had the ability to pursue healing.

I thank the various therapists, friends, and my pastor who helped me with their participation in the rituals done in my healing journey. Your support and courage to witness my pain and acceptance of me provided safety to continue working.

I thank Evan Swensen of Publication Consultants who believed enough in this book to publish it.

Foreword

The journey of healing for those suffering from Dissociative Identity Disorder (DID) is never easy. These patients, and the counselors who work with them, know all too well that the road to psychological and spiritual wholeness can be arduous. There are times when the will to preserver and maintain hope are sorely tested. For these reasons alone, Dr. Lighthart's account of her path to healing from DID is a welcomed addition to the literature in this area. In a field where spiritual and religious issues are commonplace but seldom mentioned in print, I applaud Dr. Lighthart for being outspoken about this aspect of her treatment experience.

My own work with those suffering from DID continues to confirm the Biblical adage that "the truth will set you free." For these patients this truism is both psychological and spiritual. They have to squarely confront the truth of their own life narratives, particularly those aspects that were too painful to know growing up. They also often have to grapple with God's call on their lives—can they begin to trust God to lead them through the wilderness of their own brokenness? These dynamics certainly are present in Dr. Lighthart's journey. She was not spared from great suffering as she faced her own traumatic past. Yet her faith and her openness to the guidance of God provided the anchor she needed to ride out the storms that could easily have derailed her healing. In the pages that follow, Dr. Lighthart eloquently describes an effective roadmap for healing from DID, one that relies upon the help of trained professionals, the support of family and friends, and a deep faith in God. I trust her story will uplift and inspire you in the knowledge that "with God, all things are possible."

Christopher H. Rosik, Ph.D.
Fresno, California

Preface

Little did I imagine the road to be traveled when I responded to Debra's inquiry about counseling in Alaska. Little did I know how our lives already had common ground. Little did I know what God had already put together in the past, present, and future.

Four years ago when I first spoke with Debra, all I knew was that she was moving to Alaska and wanted a peek at our profession in this state. Since that time, I learned we also have as mutual ground the incredible experience of Dissociative Identity Disorder, previously known as Multiple Personality Disorder. Our experience is from some similar, and some different, perspectives. We have in common that as therapists we both work with individuals of trauma and this diagnosis.

Our difference evolves around the fact that Debra also has the history of being diagnosed with Dissociative Identity Disorder. Her dual perspective as a therapist and a client, make her writing exceptional. Also unique is her decision to not just tell her story, but to focus on the aspects and contributions to her healing. She offers wisdom and insight directly, as well as through her choice of the segments of her life she shares. She teaches through her story and through her ownership of what has made a difference in her recovery.

It would not be fair or truthful to say that everyone who is challenged by Dissociative Identity Disorder will have the success of Debra's journey. But what is fair to state, is that there is much to be learned from Debra's journey and her ability to identify and share what has made a difference in her healing. She shares the gifts of her insight, her spirituality, her journey, not for herself, but for others to benefit. She offers hope, understanding, encouragement, and techniques for recovery. I can't imagine much finer gifts to the reader, whether you be a person searching for answers to your own trauma and healing, or a therapist looking for additional ways to help another. Debra offers much to all. The reader is offered wisdom, empathy, and hope whether you are at the beginning of your quest for healing, or somewhere further down the road.

A psychiatrist that I worked with said something very significant about Dissociative Identity Disorder or Multiple Personality. He said it troubled him that the diagnosis is often spoken of under the guise of abnormal psychology. He considered that a grave injustice for he viewed those exhibiting multiple personalities as individuals who demonstrated incredible strength and a coping mechanism that had already allowed for their survival, and as healing progressed, allowed for incredible hope and validation for abundant life after the disorder.

Debra's writing is a testimony of an incredible person, on an incredible journey, who exemplifies incredible encouragement, and hope. She takes us a step further into the spiritual aspect of healing and demonstrates the significance of that power to heal us.

We each need to do our own journey, whether we are looking to heal from trauma, helping another in the journey, or perhaps we are doing both. However, a journey becomes a bit easier, gentler, when we share the experience of those who travel before us. Debra offers the road she has traveled. We may take with us what she has learned and apply it as we choose, but without question her journey offers resources, techniques, and gifts of encouragement, hope, and abundant life.

Geraldine H. Ferry, M.S., M.A., L.M.F.T., L.P.C.

Cast of Characters

Real People

David	My therapist who diagnosed MPD and worked with me through integration. Worked together for 5 $^1/_2$ years,
Lee	My co-therapist and a counselor in David's office.
Lynn	The first therapist I saw for myself. Worked together for 18 months.
A.	A personal friend.
J.	A personal spiritual friend.
Dr. B.	One of my professors in school.
T.	A church acquaintance.

My Spiritual Family

Mary	Spiritual help.	The Mother of Jesus Christ.
Jesus	Spiritual help.	Jesus Christ.
Guidance	Spiritual help.	The Holy Spirit.

My Alters

Turtle	The one who got body and host into counseling.
Debra	The logical, analytical, skeptical, practical, factual functional one.
Debbie	The caring, feeling, listening, spiritual, expressive, helping one.
Protector	The one who guarded the safe place.
Observer	The one who directed events from the inside.
Annie	A little fun loving child who feared adults but tried to please them and be good.

Nobody	A little child afraid of everything. Purpose was to take being ignored. Later changed name to Somebody as their existence and value was acknowledged
Obstacle	The enforcer of keeping secrets. If Leesa began to weaken and talk, obstacle was to back her up. Was to challenge and discount truth. Remained unaware of physical things such as dogs, airplanes, cars, etc. Later took the name Debs.
Dee	Protector of Annie and Nobody. The one to keep the body alive.
Becky	The artist. Never dealt with anyone outside the body except David once or twice.
Nancy	Carried one level of anger. The backup for Karen. Carried pure rage. Destructive to the body.
Susan	Blind. Operated by sound. The warning, or guard when vision was not possible.
Karen	Carried a deeper level of anger. Hatred. (Nancy, Susan, and Karen clustered together.
Leesa	The keeper of secrets. Was to keep events buried.
Sleeper	Shut the body down when in physical pain.
Learner	The one who studied, attended school and retained information in the academic world. (Leesa, Sleeper and Learner clustered together).
Peter	The outdoors person. Did the work females don't do. Did the yard work helped with chopping wood, did woodwork, helped build the family house, renovated dwelling, etc.
Joker	Prankster, trickster, plotter. (Peter and Joker teamed together).
Little Nancy	
Little Susie	
Little Becky	Clustered together and fractured from Nancy, Susan and Becky to cope with contradictions of the alters.
Marian	The Core person given a derivative of Mary's name because when the splitting began, the core was given Marian protection.

Not all the alters are talked about in the book. All are listed on the maps.

Introduction

To possess knowledge of who we are, to be one complete person with self-respect and love is to be cherished. To sleep peacefully without fear, to hug without trepidation, to say "no" with dignity and self-respect is a gift every child deserves. To have our memories, remembering what we have said and done, is a gift we too often take for granted.

I say this because these are fragile aspects of our lives, easily stolen and never fully restored. What is it that robs us of these things? It is trauma, be it war, abuse, natural disaster, terrorism, medical procedures, or various crimes. If enough of any one or a combination of traumas occur, we are robbed of our dignity, respect, and childhood. Over some of these traumas we have no control, but others are preventable.

As humans we are flawed, and because we are such, we suffer. I am no different. Suffering leaves wounds and wounds leave scars. Some people wear their scars like a badge of honor; some hide their scars in shame. I belong to the latter group, and because I disguised my scars they failed to heal properly. I was so successful in hiding my scars that no one, including me, knew I had any.

In 1981, while I consulted with a psychologist, Tom, about my oldest daughter, my own battle wounds began to open. As Tom worked with my daughter and me, he became aware of my tendency to sit next to a door, a door that was not blocked in any way, so that I could "get out."

When Tom revealed this observation to me, I denied it. He tested his theory by noting that I refused to sit anywhere except next to the door, always declining any other chair offered and making my daughter move if she chose the chair next to the door before I did. One day Tom pulled his chair close to the door and propped his feet against it. I felt panic mounting, and I remember asking him to please remove his feet from the door. I also remember asking him to sit by his desk, which was at the opposite end of the room from the door. Following up on intuition and experience, Tom asked me about my childhood. I explained that it had been strict. He asked for details, but I could not provide any. I would only comment that I had very few memories of growing up. I also said "according to my parents,..." or "according to my brother,..." to introduce a story told to me about me.

Someone had left a key in the lock of a door closed long ago on a battlefield in my life, and Tom found it. He turned the key and began to open the door to my past, but instead of my allowing both of us to view my history, I fled. I became confused and lost track of our conversation. One day Tom brought a female therapist into the session with us. He introduced her to me and then opened the session with a question: "Have you ever been...?" I screamed "NO!" Even though he'd stopped before saying "raped," a voice in my head finished the sentence and the response spilled from my lips. Both Tom and the other therapist looked at me in silence. I was shocked by my response. I shook myself internally and apologized to Tom for interrupting him.

I asked him to repeat his question. He did, and this time I allowed him to finish. I politely denied that I had ever been raped. I recognized the look that passed between Tom and the therapist when I screamed at him and after my denial. It was the look I give to my children when I am thinking, "I've got my answer and I know I'm right." After my scream of denial I fled, and with my polite denial I slammed the door shut, locked it, and removed the key. It would be seven years before I would reinsert the key into that locked door and allow anyone to open it.

In 1988, at age 34, I entered therapy for myself and began to allow fractions of millimeters of my life to be exposed. What I learned was that I had been to war and survived. The war I fought was not with cannons, bombs, or guns in Bosnia, Vietnam, or Ireland. My war was in a place called home, and the weapons were words and actions. The battle was abuse. Moving away from home and living on my own ended this war.

Ending the war in my life allowed my battle wounds to heal, except that because the wounds had not been cared for properly, an ugly infection lay deep within. I chose a female therapist, Lynn, whom my pastor had recommended. She helped me slowly open the scars of my wounds, clean out the infectious pus we found, and then re-bind the wounds to heal. I believed all was well. I discontinued therapy in 1989 and went on with my life, continuing to hide these fresh scars until the day arrived when I could no longer tolerate the pain.

In 1990 I began seeing another therapist, David, to help me change harmful behaviors and reactions. Together we worked toward my stated goals of stopping my hypervigilence and fears, but I was not finding any peace or resolution to my problems. Eventually I allowed David to help me unwrap the old wounds. As the scars were exposed new streaks of infection were revealed. We went about the sickening task of reopening the wounds so they could continuously drain. As each wound was drained, David helped me administer a salve, an ointment made up of one part encouragement, one part compassion, and one part courage. This salve was the course my therapy and healing were to take. His diagnosis was Multiple Personality Disorder (MPD), now known as Dissociative Identity Disorder (DID). His prognosis was good, depending on how much of myself I was willing to commit to recovery. His treatment technique was all-encompassing. Each application of salve encouraged healing, while drawing more pus from the depth of each wound. As with any infected wound, all infection had to be cleaned out for it to heal properly.

A Rogerian style of counseling with psychodrama, spirituality, and desensitization were the tools he used to siphon off the infectious material. I contributed additional tools to facilitate healing. These were journaling, painting, sketching, and listening to music. At this writing, five years post-integration, my journals reveal a history I did not know existed, while the music and artwork that allowed me to express my emotions then now help me to remember.

I began writing this book to record my journey to mental health. I continued to write it to make myself aware of the work I accomplished and the respect, love, and confidence I found for myself. I have published it so that I can help others.

Some clients have been referred to me because they were

diagnosed with MPD. These people came in either having been told they would never get better or perceiving this to be so. How sad and false! I hope that sharing my journey will provide hope and encouragement for others, whether they are diagnosed with DID or are skeptical mental health practitioners, family members, supportive therapists, or friends who share the pain of someone struggling to heal. The road to recovery is difficult and some never make it. I successfully traveled that road, and I know people need the hope that can be found in the recovery and health of someone who has gone before them.

The information contained in this book comes from my actual healing journey. It is written in my words and from my perception of reality. While my perception of reality may have been different from that of my therapist and co-therapist, they chose to accept mine instead of trying to change it. My perception of reality is where our work began.

The images used throughout this manuscript are symbols that surfaced and repeatedly appeared in my dreams and artwork. Any artwork and prose shared in this writing belong to me unless otherwise noted. The images on the opposite page were the first to appear and were the most prominent images throughout my journey. They are metaphors for the phases of my journey and recovery.

The cracked cup without a base represents my life. It receives joys and sorrows, both of which must be lived. It is cracked because it has been broken and repaired. It is missing a base because it cannot be set down or set aside. We cannot walk away from our lives no matter how much we may wish to; the cup receives and gives.

The dolphin represents a helper, a friend to those in need. It is a guide to those seeking direction, leading them through the passage from death to life, helping them make the journey through the darkness and the unknown of the unconscious. The dolphin represents persons living in the spiritual and physical world. It needs the oxygen and air from the upper world plus the atmosphere and environment from the lower world in order to survive. The dolphin is spontaneous and free, gentle but strong.

The turtle represents survival, perseverance, and strength. It is considered a warrior. It symbolizes the union of the spiritual world (upper shell) with the physical world (lower shell), providing all that is needed for life. The shell affords the turtle a protective shelter within which to retreat and to rest at any point during its journey.

"Exposed." *The secrets kept in the depth of secrecy are being brought to the surface for exposure.*

These three symbols, when brought together, represent the healing journey that must be experienced but need not be experienced alone.

The turtle was an appropriate choice to represent my entry into therapy because before a turtle can move anywhere, it must come out of its shell. In the book Failure to Scream, Hicks refers to the turtle to drive home a point when he says, "Behold the turtle who never makes progress until he sticks his neck out." By working through therapy and writing this book, I have been and am sticking my neck out.

Before my alters and I worked together, we denied all but ourselves, refusing to admit to our multiple existences. In this book I use "we" whenever I refer to myself and my system together. I chose "we" because I accept, acknowledge, and own all the separate alters that now make up one whole person. My goal in writing this book was to provide greater understanding and a deeper level of acceptance and respect for individuals with MPD/DID , including myself. I hope everyone who reads this will appreciate our courage.

As I wrote this book, I shared it with David. After reading the manuscript he wrote me a note asking if "compassionate" was the right word to use when referring to MPD/DID. I believe "compassionate" is an appropriate word to use when speaking of dissociation because one who is compassionate has sorrow for the suffering of others.

I think I processed an instinctive sorrow and grief for what was going on in my life and used a natural ability to dissociate to cope and survive. Had I not used dissociation to cope with growing up, I probably would have killed myself. Suicide is a desperate act ending a period of difficulty but resolving nothing. A therapist displaying compassion toward a client living with Dissociative Identity Disorder/ Multiple Personality Disorder offers opportunities for resolution to the pain the client has experienced, which fostered the development of dissociation in the first place. For people using dissociation as a coping mechanism, the therapist's compassion ultimately empowers them to develop enough strength to let go of their past.

In reviewing the chart notes of my counseling sessions, I can see the dance pattern my healing journey has taken. I can see and remember the emotional tug of war as I moved back and forth between admitting and denying not only the war I survived but also the effects of that war on my life as I struggled between forgetting and remembering. Abuse in my family occurred almost daily. If I was not receiving it, I was watching one of my brothers being beaten.

People who knew I was working on this book suggested I include more details and examples of my abuse so that readers could understand what I have healed from. I added examples but in later revisions removed them, not because I was trying to avoid their reality but because they depreciated the value and purpose of my message. Instead of filling this book with reminiscences of abuse, I have chosen to provide details of how I healed. This book is written from a healing perspective. Many books are available that provide details of pain and suffering. I have my memories, good and bad, but I prefer to focus on overcoming them.

Each abusive experience offered redemptive grace, not because of what happened but because it gave me the opportunity to choose what I wanted for my life: revenge or forgiveness. I harbored anger and sorrow, but now I feel joy and peace because that is what I have chosen for myself and that is what I have worked for.

I forgive my abusers, all of them. I thank God for my parents (my abusers) because they were the best parents for me. Had I had different parents, I would not be half the person I am today.

Here is a poem one of my alters wrote a couple of years into therapy with David:

Deep Within
By Turtle

"The voices stop and silence is bliss
but my mind does not stay still.
It races to finish what will be lost before it is gone.
I am forever changing, always the same.
Retrieving unretrievable memories
will be a life-long process ending too soon.
So it is with each waking day that I sleep,
never knowing who I am within the person I have found.

If you found this paradoxical, then welcome to the devastatingly compassionate world of Dissociative Identity Disorder (DID).

NOTES

Chapter One
I Begin to Face the Truth

I first entered therapy for myself in 1988 because for more than 10 years I had carried pictures in my head of being raped. Even though I denied having been raped, I sought help because I wanted to get rid of my fears of being hugged, of being within an arm's length of another person, of feeling threatened by fat or obese people, (particularly men). I also entered therapy because I wanted to stop the belief that I caused men to touch me, to sin; that I was responsible for Mom's beating me and for other people's behavior. I would pray, begging God to change me so that other people would stop hurting me. Then I "wouldn't be bad."

In my private attempt to help myself change, I began to meditate and move into contemplative prayer. During these times of prayer I came to understand that my beliefs were incorrect, that I was not responsible for other people's behavior. I did not control the beatings from my mother or the touching by my father and other men. I did not encourage my brother's sneaking into my room or spying on me while I was changing clothes. Although I learned this in contemplative prayer, I was unable to assimilate this revelation and allow it to help me heal. In therapy I hoped to find the peace I sought and end my misery.

Therapy begun in 1988 ended in September 1989. I terminated it because I believed I had gone as far as I could, that I was "all well." In the nine months that followed the end of my counseling, life did not improve. My fears and misery continued. Pictures, sounds, and smells continued to invade my life, increasing in frequency and intensity, destroying my belief in my own sanity.

In June 1990 I "found myself" attacking an innocent person.

I say " found myself" because I felt like I had just woken. I was dazed, confused, and terrified. I looked at someone who was screaming at me to stop while she tried to pry my hands off someone else. I looked at my hands and felt sick and evil when I realized they were strangling someone. I could not seem to control them. Finally my will broke through and my hands stopped. I was appalled by my behavior. I tried to reach Lynn, but my phone mysteriously went dead every time she answered. After three failed attempts to maintain phone contact with her, I gave up. As I tried to make sense of what was happening, I remembered stories told to me by a former military roommate. She had told me that I reacted to and behaved strangely in some situations and frequently physically attacked people for no apparent reason. I had no memory of attacking people, yet I could not ignore what she had said. I also remembered my husband's telling me I had thrown him across a room, yet I had no memory of doing so. Something lay hidden in me that I had no knowledge of or control over, and it terrified me.

For several days I tried to forget what had happened, to be more aware of what I was doing, but pictures continued to flash before me. They seemed to be superimposed onto everything I was doing. One such picture was of my father penetrating me with his fingers. I felt sick and looked for a place to hide. When I saw this image I felt the physical pain and I wanted it to stop. I tried to end the flashback by closing my eyes. I stopped the picture, but I was unable to stop the sensation of pain. Then I started feeling light, as if I were going somewhere I couldn't see. My head felt as if it were being separated—one side heavier and being pulled down while the other side was being pulled up. Now I was experiencing two worlds at the same moment: one in which I felt pain, and the other in which I felt nothing. How could this be? Mentally I was gone and so were the picture, the pain and the fear. The next time I was aware of this image I refused to talk about it. I would not speak of this image as well as some others until I began seeing David.

When I saw the picture of my dad I also saw a memory of a statue in the church I had attended as a young girl. The statue was of Mary, the Mother of Jesus. She was looking at me, and tears were running down her face. She cocked her head and raised her arms toward me, beckoning me to come to her.

This was not the first time I had experienced this, nor was it the first time I thought I must be crazy, because I as well as everyone else knew that statues cannot move on their own. I had seen this statue and the image of my father in my previous therapist's office in 1988, as if it were burning a hole in her carpet. I told her about the statue of Mary, but I refused to tell her about the memory of my dad. I remember thinking I was a disgusting person, that I must be "real sick" to see my father that way. I remember that I closed my eyes then, too, in an attempt to make it go away. I remember feeling a change occurring in myself. I felt my eyes, skin, and face change. It felt good. I felt safe. I opened my eyes and things looked different, as if they were far away and I had double and triple vision. Everything looked colorless, like an old black-and-white movie. I kept trying to figure out what I was supposed to be doing.

Now, years later, I have found a comment in Lynn's notes: On August 8, 1988, she wrote, "agrees she's two people, explore." Did she suspect DID? When the picture of my dad and the statue of Mary continued to surface, I panicked and called a psychologist. I had met him only once before. His name was David.

David seemed safe and non-judgmental, so I told him what I knew of my life. Unfortunately, the majority of what I knew were memories of stories told to me about me by my family and acquaintances, while my own memories were almost non-existent. I decided to work through my recent experiences and behaviors and not go into the past at all. I set a goal to end therapy three months later, when I was scheduled to resume my college education.

The alter who carried us to therapy and represented the host was Turtle. Turtle was in a couple of dreams I had after I began therapy with David but before he diagnosed me with MPD. We chose the name "Turtle" because we believed in wholeness, and we persisted in seeking a nurturing therapeutic relationship with someone as strong as we were but also safe. We found him in David, who did not judge us.

I told David of my recent behaviors (attacking people), the stories told to me, and the flashes I saw, but I refused to tell him of the arguments and conversations I heard in my head and wrote in my journals. I also refused to tell him of the shadows in my sleep and mental peripheral vision. Not only would I not tell

David of these, but I also would not admit these experiences to myself. I was afraid that admitting they were happening would mean they were real, that I was seriously ill and would be considered a danger to others and myself. I was afraid David would have me locked away and keep me from getting my counseling degree. I was also afraid to admit to hearing conversations because I was beginning to question the appropriateness of my being in school and working toward a counseling degree. For more than 16 years I had dreamed of getting this degree.

As therapy progressed over several weeks, it seemed to me that I was making no progress, so I requested and consented to the use of hypnosis to "put an end" to what I refused to admit existed. What I expected (an end to my suffering) did not happen. Under hypnosis the arguments, shadows, conversations, and forgetfulness I had been experiencing intensified, but I still refused to tell David about them. Instead of telling him what I was experiencing, I wrote in my journals. When I read what I wrote, I was ashamed because my language, grammar, and penmanship seemed to vary as much as the conversations. My journals looked like several people had taken turns writing in them, and some of the entries were vicious and vulgar.

Things seemed to continue getting worse and finally came to a head in December 1990, three months beyond my targeted termination date (six months after my first meeting with David). I felt discouraged, angry, and hopeless.

David suggested that using a ritual would help bring the resolution I was looking for. I decided a ritual might help, so I planned a traditional one with David, myself, and a few other therapists. The ritual was an attempt to resolve my fears and let go of the past I couldn't remember but still felt haunted by. The ritual was innocent enough—or so I thought.

In preparation for the ritual I prayed, I wrote, and I listened. I prayed to God, asking Him to fill me with wisdom and direction. I wrote of my confusion and anger. I wrote prayers and a poem. I listened to the Holy Spirit provide the wisdom and direction I sought. I remember feeling hesitant when I designed the ritual and shared it with David. I worried that David would scoff at my method of praying and then my hearing from God. I feared that David would have me locked up in a hospital. I had been raised to depend on tangible senses: sight, sound, touch, and logical observation. I understood that anything else would get me locked away. Having learned to be logical and to depend on tangibles, how then did I choose to pray and listen?

When I was in 7th grade a Catholic nun presented the reality of a loving God talking to us through the Holy Spirit. And my grandmother, whose twin sister was healed of cancer from the water from Lourdes and lived to be 98, believed in a merciful God. Prior to 7th grade I was allowed to spend one week every summer with Grandma and Aunt Helen, so I was exposed to their faith and their teachings. I learned to believe in God in a way that was different from what I had been taught. Before my exposure to Grandma's faith and that of my 7th grade teacher, I thought God was a punishing God waiting to "get us" for all of our sins. Grandma, her twin sister, and my 7th grade teacher introduced me to a God of love, compassion, and mercy. This is the God who would help me heal.

I wrote the following outline as I understood the Holy Spirit directing me. I reviewed it and finally decided to give it to David. I told David he could make any adjustments or changes he thought necessary. I told him, "You have my permission to be more assertive with me to keep me from backing away or blanking out an experience."

Outline for Healing Ritual

Before starting, one minute of solitude and prayer (me).

1) Relax.
2) Play first two songs (about eight minutes): "The Warrior is a Child," by Twila Paris.
3) Read "Lost Child."
4) Play next song (about four minutes): "Honesty," by Margaret Becker.
5) Express my fears of this; give up my gift box, which contains my fears written out.
6) Try to trigger my emotions. Suggestions are sudden loud noise; mom's beatings with a shovel, belt, bat, etc; Dad's abuse of touching, masturbating, etc; the statue of Mary; touching my throat and restraining me. These items must be addressed, spoken out and not left silent. Anything else may be used such as words, phrases to help. Add affirmations as needed. Play "Hurt by Hurt," by Bill Gaither Trio.

7) The next songs (about five minutes): "The Child Remembers" and "A Time to Rest." Any more emotions?

9) Read bottom of "Lost Child."

10) Play song (about four minutes): "King of Dreams" by Chris Christian.

11) Play song (about three minutes): "I Will Go On" by Bill Gaither Trio.

Music touches deep recesses in me. I used music and song throughout the ritual to help me reach those recesses. Poems also penetrate deeply. I wrote "A Lost Child" at about 3 o'clock one morning. I was most productive in the early morning hours during which I painted, and wrote the music and poems that were important to my healing.

I struggled with putting this ritual together, and because it was so difficult for me I looked at reasons for doing and not doing this session. Some of my reasons were "I am afraid of my emotions and the power in them; I do not like my emotions; I am ashamed of my emotions; I do not want others to see my emotions" and "I am afraid of being rejected for those negative feelings; I hate my feelings and my reactions, and when they come up I hate myself."

When I copied the outline out of my 1990 journal, I noticed something else I'd written: "I fear power. It was power of the emotions and power to control that brought beatings, lost control and raped us that I feared. I fear 'Power.' By trying to hide my own power, I think I am running from it but in reality I am strengthening it." As I read this, I realized that what I had been strengthening was the explosive potential of power.

A LOST CHILD

I hear a child, I stop to listen and it is crying, not loud, but crying. I call but it answers not. Can it hear me? Can it speak, how old is it? I go in search of this child. I can't tell if it be boy or girl, 0 or 2. As I walk the cries grow quieter, then stop. I sit down to rest and I nap. I am awakened by cries again only they be louder. Again I call out, again, no answer. I start searching and again they grow quiet. I seek guidance from the Spirit of wisdom. I seek the right path and I seek aid for the child. Suddenly I am moving, drawn in a direction I don't expect. A path lies ahead. A path of thorns, underbrush, ravines and rocks, holes and fallen logs. The cries resume and grow louder. Suddenly they be next to me. I look and see nothing. Again I call to the child and there still be only cries. Be it boy or girl, 0 or 2, I still can't say, I only know it's the cry of a scared child. I again beg guidance from the Spirit of wisdom and direction. I am led to sit and sleep. Now the cries again become soft and quiet. When I open my eyes next, I see the child, she has found me. So little, so frail, so afraid. She stands there looking at me with so little trust. I put my arms around her and seek the Spirit of love to console her, hold her, care for her and love her. The Spirit helps me with me. The child has been brought home.

The date scheduled for the ritual session arrived. I was scared. I knew David and two of the other five people who were there. How would they react to the plan I wrote, which I understood the Holy Spirit would direct? One other part of this ritual I was afraid of was to having David touch my throat. I feared this because I did not think this was a normal procedure, and I could not tolerate anything touching my throat.

Things seemed to be going well. I was relaxed letting go of the things I knew and remembered, when the ritual took an unexpected turn. David touched my throat with his finger. When he did this I exploded emotionally, terrified that I was going to die. I was no longer in the present, feeling as if someone were trying to choke me. I felt hands on my throat, and all I knew was that I needed to get them off before I stopped breathing.

In reality there were no hands on my throat. I was aware of struggling and fighting to be free but seemed unable to. I saw eyes floating before me, staring at me. I closed my eyes to shut them out, and I began to feel a familiar change. I panicked. I began raging in my terror. I felt wild, out of control and unable to stop. I opened my eyes while I continued to struggle to free myself of the hands (there were no hands), to stop what I thought was happening, but I had to close them again. When I opened them once more I saw the eyes behind the hands. They were the eyes in a memory from my childhood. To shut the eyes out again I closed my eyes and erupted in a rage. Someone inside of me turned on David, whom I saw as my tormentor. This "someone" wanted to make our tormentor stop and pay for the danger we thought we were in. We thought David was a threat to our life and to us. Dee, a protector inside me, had stepped in to stop the threat. Dee existed to protect a child, Anne, and took her job and her purpose seriously. As soon as Dee recognized the danger was over, she vanished.

The look in the eyes and the hands on my throat would kill me.

At this point in my work with David, he had not yet diagnosed me with MPD. This violent outburst came as a total surprise to everyone. I was aware of fear and shame but not the violence. I had no idea I had such a potential for violence.

Initially I did not remember much of the ritual session. The memory of what occurred in this session did not come until later, when integration began. I struggled to be aware of the entire session but was only able to maintain awareness of the fear and shame.

David helped us calm down, and then ended the session. Over the next several weeks David and I continued to try to process the outcome of that ritual session, to know and understand, but the memory of the session and ritual was locked inside, away from me. At this point in therapy I did not know about DID or what fed my terror. I would soon learn about MPD and all of my alters, but it would not be until 1993 that I would be permitted by Leesa (one of my alters) to know and understand what had happened during this particular session.

The ritual session did not end therapy, propelling me instead into depression. It also thrust me into a stubborn resolve to get to the root of my problem. Little did I anticipate that counseling would continue another four years. I believe David made his MPD diagnosis shortly after, if not immediately after, the ritual session.

The conversations, arguments, and shadows in my head continued after this session. They intensified until I didn't know what was spoken out loud or what was spoken only in my head. I was also experiencing ongoing headaches. The more I struggled to sort out what was happening, the more my head hurt. The more I tried not to lose track of what was going on in my life, the more headaches I had. The headaches began taking over my sessions with David. I would go in feeling nervous, looking for an excuse not to keep my appointment, then I would leave with a major headache and feel like I was dragging myself home. Once home I would usually lie down and let my mind "disappear."

My journal entry dated June 13, 1991, noted the appearance of "Turtle," who provided me with a brief overview of my interior world and how I had survived. Turtle assured me that what I was experiencing was real, and that my not telling David would ensure my failure as a counselor. When Turtle made itself known, I decided I had nothing to lose by telling David of the secret conversations heard only in my head. I resigned myself to the fact that I was crazy and that I might never attain my (now 17-18 year) goal of becoming a counselor or psychologist. I felt hopeless and I considered dropping out of school, but an inner voice, my internal guidance (the Holy Spirit), encouraged me to remain in school and to be honest with myself and David.

Staying in school was difficult. Periodically I found myself going to the wrong class with the wrong books because I had lost a day somewhere. I would be certain it was Monday, only to find out it was really Tuesday. Then I would wonder what happened on Monday. Believing I had missed classes on Monday, I would go to school on Wednesday to discover I had indeed attended the correct classes on Monday, taken tests, and even made A's on those tests. I would have no memory of this.

After several episodes of this I became angry and was determined to quit counseling because I thought it was "messing me up." I canceled my counseling sessions through David's secretary, but David would always call me back and talk me through the crisis eventually getting me to a point where I would reschedule my canceled appointments. David always used logic and asked challenging questions about my goals and projections for my future. He reflected my goals like a mirror, and forced me to compare what I wanted to be with what I was experiencing at the moment.

One semester I had one instructor for all five of my classes. This instructor observed and noted my chaotic behavior and critiqued my work as being unpredictable, prejudiced, and rigid (even though it was all "A" or "B" work). I did not know how to explain the loss of time and memory I was suffering, so I decided to throw the truth at him. I told him I was in counseling and had received a diagnosis of MPD. He quickly ushered me out of his office saying he didn't believe in MPD. He never referred to my chaotic behavior again.

I began to see the shadows in the periphery of my sleep and mind more frequently, almost constantly. I don't think they actually increased in frequency, I think I was becoming more and more aware of their presence. They were faint, with attention-gripping behaviors of arguing, studying, sleeping, and working. Originally I didn't know what the shadows were, now I know they were my alters. One of the most irritating things to put up with in life is feeling or thinking that you have been doing something and having no memory of it. This will drive some people to compulsively document their daily activities every few minutes. I did this in an attempt to identify what I sensed I was doing but couldn't remember. I documented my days not for therapeutic reasons but to prove to myself and David that his diagnosis was incorrect. Documenting my days would become therapeutic later, however, because it proved me wrong. No matter how hard I tried, I could not account for my time each day. The only time of day I didn't document was when I was asleep. My inability to account for my time during the day was infuriating.

I didn't sleep. Each morning I was exhausted when I first woke up, and I remained exhausted throughout the day. I would fall asleep quickly at night but then sleep fitfully, aware of shadows moving throughout my head. Mine was a sleepless sleep, if such a thing is possible. No wonder I was exhausted.

Initially, only two alters, Debbie and Debra, dealt with David, and they didn't trust him. The first thing David did was to help them make a safe environment for themselves so they could feel safe in his office. David was not alone in earning their trust. Others (whom David knew nothing about) existed inside, and they, too, had to learn to be trusted. When Debbie and Debra began working with David, he had no understanding that they considered themselves separate entities with different opinions, ideas and techniques for processing information. With time, David learned the difference between Debbie and Debra, and he learned to find out which of them was speaking.

As Debbie and Debra switched back and forth working with David, I became more aware of headaches but did not understand why I had them. I noticed that my headaches became more frequent and intense during my mental conversations and arguments. David and I eventually linked them to the switching going on in me. I was learning that when I switched between alters, or when I fought switching, the headache became almost unbearable. Once I allowed the switch to be completed, the headache went away until the next switch.

Eventually, Debbie and Debra trusted David enough to allow some vulnerability. This opened the door in my mind to allow others to emerge and work with David, although Debbie and Debra refused to admit any others existed.

As David encountered more alters, my headaches intensified. I became aware of increased internal arguing and fighting as mental barriers built up over the years began breaking down. Sometimes I wanted to scream, "Shut up!" I was not aware of the alters, only the feel of them, and I refused to tell David what I was experiencing. I heard some part of me somewhere try to explain to me what was happening, but I refused to listen and accept what I heard. I denied the alters and they denied me. All of us denied our memories and we denied ourselves. I was thinking (and I heard others inside saying) that I was going insane. I accepted my thinking that I was going insane, but all the alters refused to allow anyone else to think, say, or insinuate that we either were or might be insane. No one wanted to hear that our reality existed and was healthy, or that our reality existed and was unhealthy. We especially didn't want to hear that any other part existed. Each alter had the same attitude: "I am coming out. Because I am coming out, I alone exist; therefore, I will do the telling." Because the alters were so certain of their own reality, they each took a turn at trying to prove their sanity and their sole existence. This only resulted in confusion and amnesia for everyone. It became so intense that none of us could remember what we were doing, saying, or thinking. No one inside of me could remember my visits with David, and I could not remember the alters' visits with David.

When David first addressed our amnesia and the idea of a split personality, we ignored him. Then something inside seemed to come together, and I experienced a "sigh of relief." I heard Turtle say, "I have done my job. I have found everyone, I have found help for us, and now I can leave because I know we are where we belong to get the help we deserve." It seems Turtle had grown up since I had left it in a safe place a long time ago, and it found me as well as the rest of us.

I think I had been working with David about 18 months when one of the shadows in my sleep identified herself as "Learner." This alter did my studying for school. Learner studied only at night because this was the only time there was no competition for control over our available hours. This explained why I could know information for a test when I was unable to answer questions after I'd studied. I never remembered what I knew I had read. I think Learner not only studied at night but also took the tests and attended many of my classes. I believe Learner took most of my tests because I simply did not remember having taken them.

One particular incident I do remember is when I walked into Dr. B.'s office one day to ask him for help on an assignment. As I entered he asked me if I wanted to see my test results from that morning. I can still see the confused expression on his face when I asked, "What test?" and told him I hadn't taken any tests that day. He handed me my test while informing me that I had earned the highest grade, 98 percent.

I believe Learner attended most of my classes, and one in particular. I remember signing up for a Social Psychology course but do not remember ever attending it. I later found the text and a notebook of notes from the class. I also found papers and a report of a group behavioral study I helped conduct. I had no memory of the class, the study, reports, or tests, yet I'd received only A's in this class. Later I was allowed most of the memories from this class, and I believe Learner is the one who released those memories.

Learner began helping me become aware of her studying. In my sleep I could see someone studying the textbooks. I could see her turning the pages, and I could hear her reading the words. I would wake up and discover I was in bed, with no textbooks anywhere around me. I would drift off to sleep again, and the studying would resume. When I woke for the day I would find the textbooks and look up the material I had seen Learner studying in my sleep, but I would not recognize it. Even though I had seen Learner studying, I was unable to remember or recognize the material.

Another alter identified herself as Becky. Becky was the artist, and usually surfaced at two times: at 2 or 3 in the morning, and to paint in art class. Even though Becky came out to paint in art class, she never spoke to the instructor. She communicated only through her artwork.

Becky's appearance in class caused my art instructor to wonder about me. He would try to teach me and help me develop technique, only to become exasperated because I seemed unable to understand what he said. One day I was listening to the instructor explain something when in my head I heard Becky say, "Tell him to talk to you as if you were 10 years old." I asked my instructor to explain what he was saying in terms a 10-year-old child could understand. He looked at me for a second and then granted my request. When he looked at my work about 15 minutes later he said, "Perfect, you got it perfect. Now do that all the time." I never did tell him Becky did the painting. I will talk more about Becky in chapter 4.

In my effort to speed the healing process, I attended group therapy in conjunction with individual therapy. The group offered additional support but also seemed to stir up more emotions than it settled. I found myself bracing against anticipated attacks that never occurred, until one day I almost fled from the group. What people were talking about in the group frightened me and caused a nervousness and agitation in me I was familiar with but couldn't explain. I struggled mentally and emotionally to understand my gut reactions but was unable to. In an attempt to calm my gut, I grabbed a pencil and started sketching. The relief I felt was tremendous, as if someone had opened a valve and drained off the overflow. This showed me that while I might not understand my feelings, I could begin to feel safe with them if I sketched, sculpted, or painted them.

I felt like a hole had been cut or torn in my gut. The words sliced through me opening a gaping hole.

The picture I sketched when I grabbed a pencil that first time was a knife. The relief was immediate. Today when I look at this sketch I still feel the emotions that evoked the picture, but now they are not threatening to me. I learned that painting and sketching what I could not verbalize enabled me to begin sorting, naming, and claiming my feelings. This in turn enabled me to stop forcing my emotions into hiding. Turning my feelings into art freed me to experience them in a safe context and allowed me to share them with David. After putting my feelings in the form of art, I did not feel threatened.

About this time I became aware that my dreams indicated the struggle I was going through, the fights I was having with myself, and the depth of my denial. I will share two of our dreams here as well as my understanding and interpretation of them. In the first dream I had a toilet that needed cleaning. It was filthy, full of human waste and other garbage. One top of it all was a vinyl cushion covering some neatly folded plastic bags. I couldn't bring myself to take the cushion off, so I flushed the toilet. The water level rose and pushed out the cushion and the plastic bags. The waste was now visible. The cushion and garbage bags were ugly, filthy, and untouchable. I felt like gagging and I felt sick. I just couldn't bring myself to clean up the mess, even with gloves on.

In the second dream I went upstairs to clean my attic. I found it fairly clean, with newspapers folded and stacked neatly in the corner. As I finished straightening up the rest of the attic, the pile of papers started rising and falling out of place. I rushed over to put them back, to keep them from making a mess, but they kept rising, tipping, and falling. I felt frustrated and angry. I didn't want these messing everything up. After I realized I couldn't stop the papers from falling, I gave up fighting them and just let them fall. I looked around to see what had caused them to rise. I found a plastic tube blowing helium under the pile. I jerked the tube out, but another appeared. Every time I pulled one tube out another would appear. It was as if someone were purposely upsetting things in my life. I began reading the papers and found history in them, my history.

I interpreted these dreams to mean that I was "stuffing" and trying to keep a lot of "stuff" from surfacing. I wanted to continue denying everything I was beginning to remember. I wanted to deny the reality that existed inside of me. I fought to deny the MPD diagnosis. I became angry with David if he said MPD to me; I didn't want to hear it. I even told him one day that I didn't want to hear him talk about MPD or split personalities. I wanted to keep everything hidden, but it would no longer remain buried.

Soon after I told him I didn't want to hear him talk about MPD, David gave me several insurance forms to sign. In doing this he stripped away my final resistance to the diagnosis (perhaps unknowingly). David had given me 10 to 12 forms to sign. My signature went on a line right below the diagnosis code. Every time I signed my name I could not avoid seeing the diagnosis of Multiple Personality Disorder. Each time I signed my name I felt a raw strip of pride being yanked off my insides and fresh, warm blood flowing over the wound.

The work we were doing, plus the effort expended on daily activities, was consuming vast amounts of energy, which continued to increase our exhaustion daily as well as weaken our cognitive abilities. I finally admitted to David that I was not remembering our sessions or what he was saying, that what he told me was all too bizarre. Because I consistently forgot our visits, we began video taping the sessions. These tapes further dismantled my walls of denial. On these tapes I could see the traits and behaviors my alters exhibited. I could hear what they said even though I would not remember any of it afterward. The tapes provided a backup for our sessions, so I didn't need to try to remember the sessions. I could come back to them any time I was ready.

I became angry. I wanted to prove the tapes wrong. As I continued working with David my library of tapes grew, and my ability to remember the sessions and learn about myself slowly increased. As I moved toward wholeness, my anger at myself and my alters diminished until it changed to love for myself. This love emerged after lots of fighting with myself, and cost me a lot. It cost me my fantasies about what my life had been like and forced me to face the truth.

Learning about myself and loving myself meant I had to face the fact that I could not remember my home life any better than I was remembering my counseling sessions or schoolwork. Being able to remember anything, especially daily life, was important to me, particularly since my children were using my lack of memory to get away with activities I would never condone or allow. Learning about myself and loving myself meant I finally had to let go of the image I wanted of my life and accept what I had: chaos. It also meant I needed to fully trust God to be honest with me. And since I still thought David might try to trick me it meant I had to trust David, because the Holy Spirit said David was trustworthy.

To ensure I was aware of what agreements I had made with my children, I began requiring them to sign contracts with me. I found this to be the only way I was able to know what I had agreed to, and the only way I was able to stay on top of things with my children and not doubt my sanity. I also decided to document in my journal agreements my alters made with David in session or with me in and out of sessions. We were now becoming accountable to one another.

Trying to maintain relationships as wife, mother, and student increased my stress and exhaustion so much that I began finding myself rolled up in a tight ball, crying, hugging my knees, rocking, shaking, banging my head and feeling very small. When I shared this with David he told me I demonstrated similar behaviors in our counseling sessions. I was able to verify this with the videotapes of our work together. My alters and ego states were surfacing to cope with all the stress and problems in my life, trying as they had in the past to make everything in my life work. But they couldn't do it anymore; too many walls and barriers had been dismantled.

One of the most difficult things for me to learn was to let go when an alter wanted to surface. I wanted to maintain control of what was going on, so I desperately fought "switching" (allowing another alter or ego state to take control). Unfortunately, each struggle against switching brought on intense headaches that were only relieved when I let go, relinquishing control to another. This meant mentally stepping back and out of awareness, as if in a dream, except that I was denied any awareness of who or what mentally took my place. Relinquishing this control provided alters the opportunity to express their and the system's fears, memories, and pain trapped within.

Over time David was able to help me trust the others, and together he and I helped them to trust me so that they would allow me to know and feel what they knew and felt.

Chapter Two
Acceptance

Even after David's diagnosis, I continued to deny the existence of MPD/DID, let alone the possibility that I might have it. I firmly believed DID was a bizarre, scientific concept inspired by fiction and exploited by Hollywood to rake in money. I never read the books Sybil or The Three Faces of Eve. I never watched the movie Sybil. As far as I was concerned, these were fiction, not the true stories of someone's life.

David gave me a homework assignment to work on between counseling sessions. The homework was to review the literature of MPD. I think this was supposed to help me accept the diagnosis. Since I was in a psychology program, I decided to use the homework from David to fulfill an assignment for my Abnormal Psychology class. My intent was twofold: to compile enough evidence from existing literature to demonstrate to David and myself that he had diagnosed me incorrectly, and to fulfill a class requirement to write a report on a disorder from the DSM III-R (Diagnostic & Statistical Manual of Mental Disorders, 3rd edition, rev.). I found what I believed to be sufficient evidence to dispute the DID diagnosis and presented it to David. He suggested that I might be less than objective, while also acknowledging that I might be correct.

While I worked on David's assignment Turtle took the articles, studied them, and reported being confused. The articles listed a few behaviors to look for; two of which are having clothes for someone else to wear that I wouldn't wear and having things in my possession I did not remember buying or being given. Turtle agreed that my wardrobe didn't contain clothing for people other than myself. It also agreed that I didn't own items I couldn't remember buying or being given. But Turtle then pointed out to me that the literature addressed many of the reported (what I told David about) and unreported (what I would not tell David about) experiences it knew of (a minor detail I was unwilling to recognize). I would soon discover that another alter, Observer, knew of the personal experiences Turtle was referring to and agreed that these experiences did indeed match some of the other experiences described in the literature.

I, like Turtle, remembered being called a liar by my family, who said that we "wouldn't know the truth if it hit us in the face." Turtle and Observer reported that we were constantly being accused of pretending to be someone we weren't. Both Turtle and Observer reported being aware of the conversations and arguments in our head—the very thing I denied. Knowing we could no longer hide the problem, Turtle decided it was time to take a risk. It brought us in for help and confided in David. This was the first time it ever told anyone about what we believed to be bizarre experiences. Turtle told David that whenever someone asked about those experiences it joined us in our denial, even though no one else in my system knew it existed. Turtle reported joining our denial because it, too, believed we would be locked away if anyone ever found out about the conversations and arguments. We told David that we feared being locked away, that we had heard so many times that people who hear voices, who can't remember, who lie, and who pretend should be locked away; that we thought all people, particularly therapists, believed this and would lock us up. Turtle then encouraged me to disclose our hiding place to David, saying that I needed to trust him. After my disclosure it returned inside to rest and sleep in our safe place.

During Turtle's review of the literature it helped me become aware of the reports by "experts" in the field of DID. Experts such as Bryant, Kessler and Shirar, and Putnam say that when they take a client's history large gaps in the client's memory are typical.

When Turtle retreated inside I asked the Holy Spirit to keep me from being misled and to guide me in my counseling sessions with David. Trusting David with the knowledge that I spoke to the Holy Spirit and that the Holy Spirit spoke to me was a risk I finally took. But I took that risk only after David assured me that he wouldn't "put me away."

Only one other time had I told a doctor that I spoke to God. In 1981 I told the psychologist who asked if I had ever been raped that I talked to God. This doctor raised his eyebrows, leaned toward me, looked into my eyes, and asked, "Have you ever heard God answer? "Yes," I said. "What did you hear from God?"

I told him. Then he leaned back, relaxed, and said, "Well if God said anything, that was the best thing to say." The Holy Spirit showed me my denial of memory loss. I had always prided myself on my memory and my ability to recall verbatim meetings and conversations; now my pride was stripped away. I kept running into people who reminded me of conversations I'd had with them, activities I'd done with them, and activities I was supposed to do with them but didn't.

In facing the reality of my memory loss, I became angry because I was forced to admit I didn't know what was happening in my life. I really didn't know myself at all. I was challenged to remember events in my life such as my marriage, my children's births, my sister's birth, my grandmother's death and my confirmation. Such events are important and usually unforgettable, but I couldn't remember them. I was able to provide facts such as dates of marriage and births because they were written down. Photographs elicited feelings in me but little else.

There was also a large gap in my memory of my mother's pregnancy with my sister and the four years between third and seventh grade. I know no one remembers all of her or his life, but I was 10 and 11 when my sister was born, and four consecutive years of my life is a long time to lose. Due to my lack of memory I was unable to provide any kind of consistent and chronological history of my life.

According to Putnam, this is typical. He wrote that "two features that characterize the chief complaint and past history of an MPD patient are frequent inconsistencies and lack of chronology."

The reason people diagnosed with MPD/DID lack an accurate chronological history of their life is that the alters and ego states emerge, taking up periods of time anywhere from a couple of minutes to years, and do not share what happens during those periods with any other alter. I found this hard to accept and admit about myself. I also found it hard to accept as a professional. I believed in self-control, and the concept of some alter taking away time and memory meant that maybe I didn't have as much control as I needed, or maybe I had too much control. It made me question the balance in my life as well as in the lives of other supposedly normal people.

We struggled to stay in therapy, and we did stay thanks to encouragement from David and challenges by the Holy Spirit. The Holy Spirit charged me to demonstrate the same courage I would ask of my clients, which was to learn about themselves and change what they wanted changed. When I canceled appointments, became disheartened, and began giving up, David would challenge me to look again at my goals. He would also challenge me to ask the Holy Spirit what I should do. Reviewing my goals gave me direction. Knowing that someone (David) was willing to walk with me through the minefield of my life gave me the courage to continue. Knowing the Holy Spirit was with me through this and that God was not abandoning me gave me the strength I needed not to give up my fight for wholeness.

Every time I became prideful and attempted to hide the fact that I was in counseling, that I needed help, that I was getting help, the Holy Spirit would challenge me by asking why I denied myself what I gave other people: acceptance for their humanity. The Holy Spirit said that if I could accept other people's weaknesses and humanness, then I needed to accept my own. It challenged me with the Second Commandment, "Thou shalt love Thy neighbor as Thyself." When I thought about this, I realized I had a choice. I could begin to love myself and give to myself what I gave to others—the wish for each person to be the person God created him or her to be—or I could start thinking about and treating others as I thought about and treated myself which was not very good. I chose to take my pride in my hands and make a gift of it to God so that I could be the person He created me to be.

As I continued with counseling, I began to accept my amnesia and my anger about it. As I accepted myself, my self-hatred began to disappear. As I faced my fears and admitted the truth, my therapeutic progress sped forward in remarkable ways, spurred by self-love, acceptance, and deepening affection among the alters. As my anger disappeared I was capable of experiencing the anger, fear, and other emotions of my alters, thus enabling me to learn about them without feeling threatened.

Freedom from self-hatred and fear allowed healthy scabs to seal old wounds, making my healing genuine. As my system learned to trust David and I let my defenses down, the alters began reporting other experiences such as running into people who seemed to know me but whom I did not know or remember, and driving to places other than where I had planned to go to.

I continually struggled with feelings of hopelessness, inadequacy and shame as memories of my life surfaced. I became more aware of how much I was "in the dark" about what had happened and was currently happening in my life. I fought against thinking and believing I was getting worse. I used logic to keep alters from "going after David" to shut him up, and to make him feel what we felt, what I felt. I would get angry with David, but I refused to tell him of my anger because he was helping me through this. I would get angry with myself for letting him help me. I would especially get angry at the Holy Spirit because it knew me better than I knew myself and used its knowledge and wisdom to hold a mirror up for me to look into. I didn't want to see what could be and what was becoming. What I saw was good. To see what was good meant I had to let go of lifelong beliefs about myself. When I let go of false truths—that I was "worthless, a nothing, a fraud, a necessary evil, an inconvenience, a something"— it became time for my alters to do likewise. Together we learned to free ourselves from these lies. It was hard work and I was getting tired.

I listened in wonder as my alters spoke of watching us do things that I myself was unable to control. I heard the panic and fear in their voices when they shared those experiences. I questioned whether I was "losing my mind," and I again sought reassurance from David that I would not be locked away, that he would not hospitalize me.

I began to feel haunted by an unfamiliar song that played over and over in my head. One day out of frustration I sat down and wrote out the music. I listened to the music and words playing over and over until I had written the melody; then I played it on my dulcimer. I realized an alter must have composed this because I did not, and still do not, know how to read or write music. As for playing music, I pick out notes, playing by ear.

Initially this song didn't mean anything to me, except that I could feel it pulling at something inside of me when I played it or sang it. I shared this song with David and he kept it in my file. One day as I was preparing to leave a session, David pulled out the song and played it on his trumpet (one of many instruments he kept in his office). The song ripped through me as if I had caught my arm on barbed wire fencing. I felt my emotions being torn open and I began crying. I could not explain why I was crying or what I was crying about; I just couldn't stop crying. This song had torn off another scab to reveal more infection underneath. As I heard the notes, the words came to mind. I cannot share the words

This music initially brought pain out in the open. Then, it helped me to feel stronger and comfortable.

here because they are in my prayer language, which is not English and which was meant only for myself and my alters.

Our song turned out to be a song of grieving, healing, and comfort for me, calming my fears, soothing my spirit, and bringing me hope again. Something I noticed after this song became a part of my work was that I no longer needed to seek reassurance from David that he would not have me locked up in a hospital.

I am still attempting to sort out what I have experienced and what I have been privileged to study. I still run the gamut of emotions and thoughts, from shock and disbelief to acceptance and acknowledgment, but never again have I taken the stand of absolute denial since I confronted MPD/DID in its real and covert form.

My lack of open-mindedness and my need to ease my anguish had caused me to overlook the covert aspects of DID addressed in the literature: that the purpose of DID is to create alter personalities to hide and protect the individual. Up to this point I had paid attention only to the literature that addressed overt indication such as differences in clothing and hairstyles, and the drastic changes in behavior. The only overt indication that I or my alters demonstrated was a drastic change in behavior, or so I had been told. I had been in the military during the 70s, and my roommate had told me people were afraid of me because I would change from pleasant to violent in an instant. Once, when I was recovering from a bi-lateral bunionectomy, a male friend and I were joking around and he did something that caused me physical pain. I responded instantly by swinging my crutch at him, tearing a hole in his leg where a wing nut on the crutch gouged him. My roommate also told me I attacked my female commanding officer one day when she startled me. A friend, who would later become my husband, confirmed my roommate's reports. He told me that many people were afraid of me and nicknamed me "the bear." He told me he was cautioned not to date me because I would kill him. Guess what? He is still alive 25 years later, even though I reportedly threw him across a room when he startled me one night shortly after we were married.

I didn't believe people when they told me of my behavioral changes: that I would be calm and pleasant one minute, then attack someone the next. Apparently, this happened often. I was made aware of this behavior one day a few years ago after church services. I was standing outside the church, speaking with an acquaintance whom I will call "A." Her children and mine were with us, and the rest of the congregation were standing about, visiting. I saw "T," a young man I knew, walking toward us. He was friendly, and I enjoyed working with him during our services. I heard him call my name. The next thing I was aware of was that I was looking at him with my arms raised as if to attack him. I heard a faraway voice say, "I'll kill you". "T" looked terrified. The congregation watched me in silence. I felt confused and as if I had just been "bad." "A" was staring at me. I asked her what was happening, and she told me that "T" had yelled my name as he jumped at me and grabbed my arm. She went on to tell me that a strange look came over my face, that I turned, raised my arm, and yelled at him that I would kill him. I apologized to "T" and drew him aside to explain that I was living with Post-Traumatic Stress and that I hadn't meant to scare him. I couldn't tell him I had been diagnosed with MPD. I calmly asked him not to jump at me or grab me again. He assured me he would never do that again, and he never has. I was angry, but I couldn't be angry with him. He didn't know about my startle response. He didn't know about my having been awakened some nights by Mom beating me with a belt or of my having been tied up (if the stories told by my family were true). He didn't know that I had been hit repeatedly on my back and on my head. I couldn't be mad at him, yet I wanted to be mad at someone. I wanted to punish someone. He didn't know and I couldn't tell him. Nobody knew except David.

This was only one incident that occurred well into my work with David. Other, similar incidents were reported to me by acquaintances and my family. I knew I needed to learn to trust myself enough to stop this behavior and get at the root of the problem.

After I built a trusting relationship with and among my alters, they began allowing me to view my video-taped therapy sessions. Up to this point, I had been reviewing the tapes but remembered nothing, as if I had never watched them. I usually fell asleep during the review. I learned, after the alters began to trust me, that falling asleep was a coping mechanism I demonstrated whenever I experienced intense pain. I invited a spiritual friend, "J," whom I trusted, to review the tapes with me. I hoped that by doing this with her I would remember them better. I didn't! I began to remember the tapes only when the alters trusted me enough to let me remember them. Slowly I began to remember what was on the tapes. This enabled me to start remembering my sessions with David.

Initially, "J" pointed out what I had denied: that my voice and facial expressions changed during the sessions. I looked and listened for suggestions planted by David, expecting to find them. I found none, and when I asked "J," if she found any, she reported finding none. Slowly I began to accept the different expressions I saw and the voices I heard on the tapes, and I was shocked. I found each facial expression and voice to be consistent with the various reported ages of the alter who seemed to be talking. The language usage, vocabulary, understanding and sentence structure were also appropriate for the reported age. I came to recognize the alters by their behavior, posture, voice, and vocabulary.

David and I tried to discuss the therapy sessions with the alters, but they remained amnesic of my sessions. I learned that alters remaining amnesic of sessions is typical. This is another reason David had suggested taping our sessions. He hoped that if he taped the counseling sessions my alters would begin working together to remember.

Studying the video tapes helped me appreciate the strength, virtue, and courage of my system as we learned about one other and about my life. We all learned we were really one person instead of many, and we began to accept ourselves as one whole person. I was always exhausted after a session, and it was not until I was allowed to observe my sessions that I understood the depth of work I and my system were doing.

The most productive sessions David and I had were those that lasted approximately 1 and 1/2 hours in the evenings. By the end of the day my system was too tired to bother fighting David, the Holy Spirit and Mary, or therapy. Sometimes I would be so tired that I didn't care how much I hurt; I simply wanted peace and was usually willing to do anything the Holy Spirit and Mary directed me to do to get that peace.

Approximately nine months after I began accepting the work I was doing as well as the reality of my life, I wrote another report on DID, this time an objective one. In this report I made no attempt to qualify or disqualify anything about DID. This objective report was a turning point, not only in my healing but also in my approach with clients, when I began respecting the clients' point of reference or point of reality and meeting them in their perception of reality. Nowhere in my classes did I recall being educated about the clients' reality, only their misperceptions, breaks with reality, and ill-formed ideas. I began to realize what I would need to do to be a therapist who is capable of helping clients achieve their goals; that is, to view myself and my clients from a "what is right and healthy" mentality instead of from a "what is wrong with me or them" perspective. I would have to accept the clients and all they would present to me. Likewise, I would have to accept myself and all that I would present. I would have to be open-minded enough to use my clients' beliefs to help them attain their stated goals and idea of healing, and I would have to be open minded enough to use my beliefs to help myself. I had to do this without condoning inappropriate and/or illegal behaviors, while at the same time refraining from passing professional judgment on myself or on my clients. I was truly beginning to treat myself with love and respect.

As I was allowed to see more and more of myself and my gifts of courage, perseverance, and faith, I began to see that God had a purpose for my life other than to suffer. I began to evaluate my life, finding a new level of respect for myself as well as my alters. I began to recognize the compassion and love I had for all of life. I also began to view therapy as a place where a lot of teaching and learning occur in both the client and the therapist.

I regret having destroyed my biased report on DID. It would be interesting to compare that report, written in 1991, to my objective report written in 1992, to see the progress I had made.

NOTES

NOTES

Chapter Three
Spiritual Help

When I brought the whole system in for healing, I knew we would not be alone. Because I knew God and had talked with Him throughout my life, I decided to invite God and the Holy Spirit to accompany us through our work with David. We needed to feel safe before we could tell David of our conversations with God, and asking God to accompany us was the only way I knew to face my fear of disclosure and vulnerability.

When David first asked if I had a safe place inside where I could go to, I asked him what he meant by a safe place. David explained that the safe place was a place I could think about inside my mind like a meadow or stream where I could mentally go to and feel safe. I said no. The concept of a safe place was foreign to me. I didn't know how to think of a safe place because everything I thought of reminded me of danger. David suggested we try to use hypnosis to help me create a safe place. I considered his suggestion of using hypnosis to help us find a safe place. I decided to push past my fear of hypnosis and use it. Inviting the use of hypnosis did not come easily. I had wrestled with my feelings about hypnosis for nearly 15 years. My husband was interested in it, but I was afraid of it. In seventh grade I had been at a Halloween party where some of the kids were experimenting with seances and levitation. What I witnessed during these experiments scared me, and I called my parents to come and get me. The altered states of consciousness I witnessed in seances and levitation reminded me of the altered state in hypnosis and I had been afraid of it ever since. Even if I ignored my fear of hypnosis, I still had to contend with what I had heard Christian churches preaching since 1974, that hypnosis was evil and the use of it would make us vulnerable to evil influences. I also had to contend with seeing it used for entertainment purposes in television.

Until the early nineties I had never taken the time to learn about hypnosis. Because of the field of work I had chosen, I needed to resolve my fears and doubts about hypnosis. I finally resolved my dilemma when I prayed to the Holy Spirit for wisdom. I was told in prayer that hypnosis is a natural phenomenon, although it is not often recognized as such. I understood that humans move in and out of trance states daily when they watch television, read books, daydream, and drive. I further understood that hypnosis administered under the proper direction would not harm me. I asked specifically if I could trust David's hypnotizing me. The answer I understood was that David was safe, that he would respect my fears, thoughts, and beliefs. I also understood that no one could make me say or do anything I would not do outside of a hypnotic trance if precautions were taken. I was told I was to take Jesus and the Holy Spirit with me in hypnosis.

As David helped me with a hypnotic induction, he suggested I invite Jesus and Mary (his mother) to accompany me. I took this as confirmation that I could trust him since, to my recollection, I had not told David that the Holy Spirit had given me similar advice in prayer. I asked Jesus, Mary, and the Holy Spirit to help me create a safe place. Mary instructed me to return to the mountains of Wisconsin, to trails I knew so well but had forgotten. When I returned to those trails mentally, emotionally, and spiritually, I found safety. I returned to paths I used to walk when I needed or wanted to hide from my family. I revisited the old creek bed, which still had only a trickle of water running through it. I remembered my pleasure in letting my horse graze by the water while I sat or lay down, listening to the sound of the water and smelling the fragrances of plants, worms, dirt, water, and air. In that special place, I could hide and relax. I could spend time with God and know that I was safe. In that place, during my childhood, the Spirit of God had told me that I would one day know a special love I was being denied. In that place I could let my mind drift, and sleep without fear. I had felt safe in those mountains among the timber wolves, deer, bobcats, rabbits, and chipmunks. When I revisited those mountains and traveled the familiar paths with Jesus, Mary, and the Holy Spirit, I felt all was well. I would gladly return there to work on my healing journey.

"Safe Place." This place is where alters began meeting each other and began trusting each other. Some caves can be seen. This is where alters disappeared to hide.

My ability to relax deeply and dissociate made it easier to reach our safe place. We soon learned we did not have to use hypnosis or dissociation, we could just close our eyes and think about being there whenever we wanted to visit the safe place. Initially, each alter explored our safe place believing that he or she was the only one who had access to it. Once an alter felt safe, it was time to begin learning about the others. Each learned that the others shared the safe place because it was created for everyone's use. When all the alters knew they were safe, they allowed David to begin learning how we functioned, how we made it through each day. I told David how Mary had reached out for me when I was a young girl, how God had spoken words of encouragement to me when I needed them most. I told him about God's telling me that there was a love for me I could not understand or know because I had never been free to experience it, but that one day I would experience it, and when I did I would recognize it.

I met with the Holy Spirit, Jesus, and Mary. They gave encouragement and wisdom. I meet with them to learn.

I came to understand that I learned things like how to take care of myself; how to take care of children; how to care for some injuries; wild foods safe to eat without studying, by going into a contemplative state with God and spending time with the Holy Spirit. I came to understand that each one of us would pray to learn and understand, and that God's Spirit honored our prayers and taught us. David encouraged each alter to work with Jesus, Mary, and the Holy Spirit. I believe that the honor and respect God, David, and I showed my alters set them free to respond to the healing being opened for us.

God has been faithful. He has revealed the special love He promised I would know: It is His love for me, combined with my love for myself. He continues to teach me about people, healing, and truth, and I continue to learn. At first I was afraid that when I no longer dissociated I would lose the ability to meditate and relax deeply, but I haven't. I had mistakenly paired dissociation with meditation and relaxation. Now I understand the difference between them.

Prior to using a meditative state for therapy, I had used it when I needed to learn problem-solving skills and parenting skills that needed to be different from those my family had used when I was growing up. I also used it whenever I was in tremendous pain and needed relief. In this place with the Holy Spirit I would be free of pain and weakness. I could rest and feel whole. Today I continue to use this state for these needs. I also use it to seek direction in work with my clients. I use this state to receive the Spirit's strength to do what It directs. During counseling sessions when I would not or could not relax and feel safe, David would probe to determine if we had invited Mary and Jesus or the Holy Spirit to accompany us to the safe place. Usually I would ask them to come with us, but sometimes I would forget to ask, or I would refuse to allow them to join us. When we brought Mary, Jesus, or the Holy Spirit to the safe place whenever I was in tremendous pain and needed relief, their presence soothed us. Whenever I brought them on the paths to our safe place their presence calmed us. In this place with the Holy Spirit I would be free of pain and weakness. I could rest and feel whole. Today I continue to use this state for these needs. I also use it to seek direction in work with my clients. I use this state to receive the Spirit's strength to do what It directs.

Many times I would go to the safe place and then sleep while another alter worked with David and our spiritual support. Mary and the Holy Spirit usually had to work with the different alters before the alters would willingly work with me. In our safe place were many places where we hid, and a kind protector alter who guarded them. The only thing we feared then was simply being discovered. When we started using the safe place in therapy, we used it as a place to hide when we felt threatened and in danger. One of the first lessons I had to learn was that the safe place truly was safe. As I climbed the paths I thought anyone below looking up would be able to see me, follow me, and discover my safe place. David asked questions to learn whether I was safe from the prying eyes of nosy people. The questions challenged me to investigate the surrounding terrain and see that it cloaked me from potential viewers. Another lesson I learned was to trust Mary and Jesus when they encouraged me through trails in which I found fear. The safe place was dark since it was deep in the woods; I did not venture into areas less well known to me.

At one point I had a dream that showed me how God's spirit was encouraging me. In the dream I was hiding in a cave. God entered the cave and encouraged me to come out. When I came out He took my hand and began leading me along a path. I became scared, jerked my hand free from His, and ran back to the cave. God returned to the cave and coaxed me out again. We resumed walking, hand in hand. After walking farther than I had the first time, I became frightened again, jerked free, and ran back to my cave to hide. Again God came to the cave and coaxed me out. This scene recurred many times, but two things would change. First, each time I walked with God we walked farther away from the cave. Second, the distance between the cave and where I would jerk free from God seemed to shrink with each scene. I discovered that as God and I were walking, the cave seemed to always be right behind me, as if following me, accessible until I no longer needed it because I had overcome my fear.

As we began to accept healing the safe place turned into a classroom and the lessons were self-acceptance and self-love. We learned we were good and valuable and had a purpose. As we accepted ourselves and our purpose for being, the safe place became less and less important to us. We could still run to our respective spots and hide, and we still learned there, but the safe place was changing. It seemed to be releasing us to seek deeper healing. As the safe place assumed a new purpose, it began being drawn toward, or was drawing to itself, a place of brilliant light. As the place of light and my safe place drew closer, we were able to move between the two places with the help of the Holy Spirit or Mary or both. We discovered we liked the light we were being offered. We learned to trust the light,

The safe place and a place of light were coming together and we wanted to stay there. It was pleasant, inviting, and healing.

and we wanted to spend more time in it. The safe place was still available to us, but we wanted the brilliance of the light and the freedom it offered more than the protection and familiarity of the safe place. As the alters began to thrive in the light, integration became the goal. We no longer wanted to "just stop" the pictures and memories or stories. We each wanted to be one whole, complete person. To do this we had to face our fear and our pain. Accepting the truth about our life and wanting to heal caused extraordinary pain, more than we thought we could bear. But the safe place and the light merged, providing us with security so we could face the next steps.

One of my earliest experiences with this light came when I would not and could not allow myself to feel and express my grief at the abuse I knew of. Mary invited me to accompany her. She guided me to a body of water, then walked out into it and waited for me to join her. I struggled to remain on land but finally went to her after a lot of encouragement from David to listen to her, to trust her, and to allow myself to receive what she wanted to give me. When I reached her she embraced me. I started crying. Her hug felt so good, so safe, and so comforting. It reminded me of the hugs my grandma gave me until my parents forbade me to have her attention. I remembered having experienced this same kind of comfort every time I put myself in God's hands when I hid from my family. Mary looked into my eyes and I saw deep love and sadness in her eyes, the same love and sadness I had seen in the eyes of a statue. I cried in her love and touch. I felt myself melt into her embrace. This was the first time David saw me cry. It was the first time he heard me speak with emotion, without the journalistic, factual style I had always used.

When I put this book together, remembering the work we did, reviewing the growth and effects it had on my life, the pain was real but without the agony of just a few years before. I experienced the continued healing God had promised. My life was no longer shrouded in darkness. My writing shed renewed light on my desire for clearer vision and understanding. The old scars were no longer bandaged and bound from sight. All signs of infection had disappeared. The scars were clean and would always be tender. One result of all this work is that I, too, have learned to carry my scars as a badge of honor. I am no longer shamed by my life. I am proud of my life because it made me who I am today. Had I had a different life, had I had different parents, I would not be half the person I am today. For that I thank God.

At times, something happens to remind me of my battle wounds. I feel my own wounds when I hear a parent tell their child they are worthless or I hear that a child was beat to death by a parent. I remember some of my own wounds when I see a child covered in bruises, see casts on broken bones, or see a child in the hospital as a result of beatings, neglect and abuse. There are times, I need to rest from the pain people inflict on one another. At times, the injuries that contributed to the development of my MPD flare up or the permanent damage done to my body drags me down. At times, I would rather die than continue feeling the pain in my body, but I go on just as I did in counseling, working to be one whole person who loves herself. I rest in the light of a contemplative state to receive relief, strength, and encouragement. I rest to receive relief from tender but healed wounds. I rest in a state I used to run away to, only now I do not run away. The light of this state stays ever around, before and with me because without it I cannot go from one day to the next. Without this light, faith, and trust I cannot listen to clients or help them heal.

In my work toward wholeness, I developed a quirk that warned David and me (if I paid attention) when neither I nor my alters were willing to do any work. I noted earlier that I did most of my therapeutic work with the Holy Spirit and Mary. I only had to close my eyes and think about the safe place and I could go there. What I did not mention was that I sat in a particular chair when I worked in the safe place. I became so accustomed to this chair that I could mentally vanish if I sat in it and closed my eyes. The quirk I developed was that I would sit on the sofa instead of the chair whenever some of us didn't want to work or do anything in the counseling session. David did not let me get away with this. He learned to address why we were refusing to work.

Sometimes I would refuse to listen to Mary and the Holy Spirit or to invite them to a session. David did not let me get away with this either. He would challenge me as to why I would not listen to them or did not want them present. When I allowed them to be with us and when we listened to them, they always encouraged us in our journey. I learned that my refusal to invite the Holy Spirit to work with me and my refusal to listen to it occurred whenever I denied the DID diagnosis. Each time this happened I was led through an internal nudging to review more literature. As I followed through and reviewed more literature on DID, I read information that seemed to confirm or validate the alter or experience I was denying.

At times, my system became so enraged with the diagnosis, the switching between alters, the headaches, and the loss of time that we would refuse to relax or cooperate with David. When these times occurred he simply suggested we ask Mary or the Holy Spirit what we needed right then. The gentle but firm voices of Mary and the Holy Spirit were the hardest to ignore because their voices and their presence wrapped us in a cocoon of love and protection while telling us truth. They never ordered us. They encouraged us to risk the truth and identify the rewards. They always left us with a choice either to risk or not to risk. Eventually I would listen to them and take the risks, which resulted in the Holy Spirit and Mary gently guiding us toward our goal of health and wholeness.

This has continued in my post-integration work. Periodically I have found myself refusing to work on this book or a new memory, and inevitably I heard the Holy Spirit challenge me to once again risk the truth and find the rewards. I wanted to believe that once post-integration counseling ended my healing would be finished, but I knew better. I have learned that my healing continues daily if I allow it. Recently I suffered a setback because I did not pay attention to stresses that were building in my life and I reverted to old coping skills. The only way for me to recover was to risk the reality of the experience and learn about a surfacing memory. I finally listened to the Holy Spirit and accepted the invitation to heal another memory. I was rewarded with new knowledge of my life and new healing. As a therapist I found this a humbling experience, one I often walk through with my clients.

As I and some of my alters reviewed the literature on DID, we found supporting comments from other therapists and experts in the field of dissociation on the presence and use of a spiritual source in the treatment of DID. One example comes from Bryant, Keesler and Shirar. They found that once the spiritual source is tapped into, therapists do not feel so alone and helpless. They have a source of assistance that can provide accurate, effective direction in their work with their clients.

I don't know how David experienced my spiritual helper. He has commented that at times he felt lost as to what to do or suggest next, so he would look to what he called the Guidance in me for direction. I don't know if he honored my use of it because it was a part of me or because he believed there was any reality to it. Maybe I'll ask him some day. What I do know is that his honoring it helped me. I found my spirituality and my spiritual helper to be the one stabilizing force in my otherwise chaotic world, and David possessed enough wisdom to use this deep part of me. According to Bryant, et. al., "The spiritual part is something within that gives the Multiple an anchor even in the midst of utter chaos—something on which she can focus, something to cling to."

As I studied and reviewed our sessions on tape, it was interesting to note that when we followed the guidance of the Holy Spirit and Mary, we healed, we progressed. But when we ignored them, we experienced setbacks and a deterioration of daily functioning. Sometimes, alters wanted to damn David for his astuteness and his ability to remember the directions the Holy Spirit and Mary gave us. I never told him all the directions I was aware of, but David would hang on to whatever I told him and challenge me with it weeks later. One such incident was during a time of emotional and physical danger. I had had to file a report on a family, and one member of the family began shooting our animals. My family became targets of harassment, and a chance existed that one of us would be physically harmed since one of the family members was already being charged with murder. I understood what I needed to do, yet I could not move myself to do it. I didn't follow the directions of the Holy Spirit because I thought the directions I understood—to move my family to a new location-would make things worse for them, and I didn't want to do that. Moving would mean giving up my home, which I would own free and clear in two years. It meant taking my children out of the only schools they had attended. David remembered what I received from the Holy Spirit and challenged my obedience to it. When I finally followed through on what I understood I should do, the danger ended. Not only did the danger end, but the house we rented was also surrounded by the homes of several police officers. I didn't know police officers lived throughout the neighborhood as well as next door and across the street until my neighbors arrived home from work the day I moved in. Talk about protection, I had it!

It seems that when I most wanted to ignore the Holy Spirit, and when I most wanted David and sometimes Lee to forget a directive by the Holy Spirit, some bit of scripture would come to mind. When I most wanted to ignore the Holy Spirit, I thought of John 16: 12-13. In this passage I was, and still am, reminded that the Holy Spirit would not mislead me.

I loved traveling with Mary and the Holy Spirit to my safe place, which was coming together with the light I experienced. I described the light (the warmth, coolness, energy and protection) to David and Lee, but I don't know if they could grasp the intensity and pleasure of it. In this place I learned, I rested, and I felt no pain or danger. My healing went deeper into my being as we progressed. My safe place and the light became one; it was here that final integration would take place, but until then I enjoyed it while I worked in it. The Holy Spirit told me I could come to this place to heal, rest, and learn, but I could not use it to run away from my problems or from healing. It was strange to have a place without judgment, fear, and cruelty. It was wonderful to be able to let go of my vigilance and have permission to relax. I now accepted that my spiritual help had sustained me, helping to keep me, as well as my system, alive.

My spiritual support provided the deep inner core to protect and sustain the person I was created to be. As all of my alters shared their stories, memories, pain, and strengths, we began our journey to the core of who we all were as one person. This core would be the final site for our integration, where we would become the one person we sought so hard to be.

Below is a sample of how David and I worked with my alters. This is part of a transcript from one of my sessions. Various alters were coming out, and David was encouraging each to work with the Guidance and Mary. What is written is verbatim from a tape of the session and begins about 30 minutes into the session.

Debra - And um, I just wish I could remember the dream. But then I was sitting out there and I was working on my scenario for ethics class and flipped my notebook paper over to get another sheet, a clean sheet, and I came across those pages there that I had written over the weekend, but I do not know how I got these in my folder because I don't remember putting them in my folder. I don't remember writing some of this.

David - But it was your handwriting?

Debra - Basically, yeah. I can't...I started reading it when I went to get the paper and I saw this instead and I could not figure it out, but it has (something) about '   Nancy and I am just not...I guess right now I feel really ridiculous.

David - Well you have a lot of stress on you and a lot of pressure so you dissociated again. "You feel ridiculous sounds like you are back where you started from in a sense. So not remembering things is like the left hand doesn't know what the right hand is doing."

Debra - I feel like I am going in every direction all at once and not really accomplishing anything, although I know I finally accomplished getting a house. I am accomplishing getting everybody where they have to be and even though I do not remember doing some of it I am still getting it done.

David - But are you talking about accomplishing your inner work?

Debra – I'm not getting anything done there. I mean, I'm not even really sleeping again at night and today I found bruises all over my legs again and I think, how did I get bruises all over my legs? I don't know how I did it. I guess I have just gotten reverted back to the only coping abilities I had and I don't like that...it is not what I wanted.

David - Right. Well, can you still remember that there were a few weeks there when you felt integrated and together, you had a different way of relating to the world?

Debra - Yes.

David - Can you remember that?

Debra - Yeah, I remember that.

David - So what was that like?

Debra - What was it like? I felt like finally I am getting somewhere. Finally I feel like I am a person instead of a thing. I felt whole. I didn't feel so scattered and afraid. I didn't feel as afraid. I remember feeling a lot of confidence.

David - So that frame of mind you are able to maintain until you are under extreme stress and pressure from the outside and you kind of reverted back into the old way.

Debra - Yeah.

David - So what you want now is to get back to that new way. Like you said last time, maybe through this you are gaining more strength and more wisdom to be able to maintain it for a longer period of time. That will help you feel safer, and maybe you can forget about all those other things and concentrate on yourself. But I'm wondering, the thing is that once you move and you feel like you really did protect yourself, and all these years with all the things going on, you just kind of put up with it. Things are really different now because you are doing something about it. So do you think that will give you some feeling of real confidence that you really could do something?

Debra - What did you just say?

David - I said, for years lots of things have been going on and you have just kind of put up with them—that were really dangerous and not healthy, or whatever, and now you are really doing something to take care of it. You are truly protecting yourself and your family in a real way. That should give you real confidence. Can you imagine after you have moved into the house? The girls are happier, you feel safe, can you imagine that?

Debra - I can't ever imagine feeling safe.

David - You can't because right now you feel very unsafe again. You are feeling all kinds of emotions right now—fear, sadness.

Debra - Yeah.

David - Who do you feel like you are now?

Nancy - Right now I feel like Nancy.

David - What do you think it is that you want, Nancy? (long silence)

Nancy - I don't know what I want.

David - Are you feeling very sad now?

Nancy - A combination of sad and angry.

David - Do you know what you are sad about or what you are angry about?

Nancy - No.

David - So it is just a general sadness and anger?

Nancy - (crying) I don't know how to say it. I don't know words for it.

David - You don't know the words to express your feelings?

Nancy - It is like if you were to cut a hole it wouldn't go down deep enough to find it.

David - You mean with feelings permeating your entire being? It is like a total feeling. Is it something you feel you can tolerate or something that is intolerable?

(Long silence, Nancy begins to cry)

David – What's happening now?

Nancy - I don't know. I'm getting a headache and I feel a lot of energy moving through my arms. Almost like I'm on edge.

David - Are you still Nancy?

Debra - No.

David - Who are you now? Debra - I don't know, I'm kind of in between.

David - Are you moving towards someone else?

(long silence)

Debra - Yes.

David - Who are you moving towards?

Debra - Lisa

David - Lisa? Are you starting to feel like Lisa now?

Lisa - Yes.

David - What do you want, Lisa?

Lisa - I would like to help Nancy but she won't let anyone help her.

David - Is there anyone there that you can ask for guidance about what is the best thing to do to help Nancy?

(long silence)

David What's happening now?

Lisa - This feeling like, I don't know, it just feels like I have been tied up.

David - Like your wrists have been tied?

Lisa—(whispering) No.

David - So is that something that happened to you, did someone tie you up?

(long silence)

David – What's happening now?

Debra - I've just got a headache.

David - Are you still Lisa? Who are you now?

Debbie - Debbie.

David - So do you remember, Debbie, that Nancy was talking to me for a while, and then Lisa for a while? Do you remember that?

Debbie - I remember Lisa.

David - You don't remember Nancy? Was there some way that you could contact the guidance now and ask for help and guidance in the process? Ask the guidance what needs to happen now to move you in the direction of becoming whole again and becoming confident again.

Debbie - I don't know what we need to do.

David - Can you ask for guidance?

(long silence)

David - Is the guidance there?

Debbie - Yes.

David - Can you get an answer from the guidance?

Debbie - Nancy is feeling very alone, she feels like she is not needed or wanted. She just needs to be wrapped up as if she was in a blanket or cocoon to protect her.

David - The guidance wants you to protect her? To wrap her in a cocoon? Who's going to do that?

(long silence)

Nancy - I just want to go out and smash lights.

David - Who are you now?

Nancy - Nancy.

David - You want to smash lights?

Nancy - I want to go out and break all the lights.

David - Which lights?

Nancy - The lights that shine on us.

David - Because you're angry at the neighbors?

Nancy - But I can't do that, it is against the law. Pat and Debbie both tell me I can't do it.

David - Do you understand why they are telling you that?

Nancy - I understand it but I don't like it.

David - Yeah. You're just angry; I mean, you feel really frustrated that you have to obey that rule. So you think you would feel better if you could just go and smash the lights.

Nancy - I'd like to sit out there with a ...with a gun and shoot when they come in the yard too. That would make them stop. But I can't do that either.

David - Do you understand why?

Nancy - It's against the law. I hate the law.

David - You hate the law, but you feel like you will obey it?

Nancy - Yes.

David - You don't want to go to jail or anything like that, right?

Nancy - No. I can't go to jail. I can't get locked up.

David - How do you feel about Debbie and Lisa? Are they all around you now? Are they near?

Nancy - They're here.

David - How do you feel towards them?

Nancy - I want to cry when I look at them.

David - Is that okay, to cry?

Nancy - No, it is a sign of weakness.

David - Who says that crying is a sign of weakness?

Nancy - We were all raised with that, with weakness and manipulation.

David - So your parents told you?

Nancy - That's what Debbie's parents told us.

David - So you believed Debbie's parents? Are they wise, kind, loving people? Do they teach you the right things?

Nancy - They are supposed to be. I don't like them.

David - You don't like them? So do you...

Nancy - I would like to beat them through a wall myself.

David - So maybe you don't have to listen to them. Could it be that it is okay to cry, it is not really a sign of weakness?

Nancy - Sometimes I start to cry.

David - Then what happens when you start to cry?

Nancy - Strange feeling, funny feelings go through me and I don't know how to handle them.

David - Do you feel like you need help? Do you need someone to comfort you or something?

Nancy - I don't feel like it is safe to cry.

David - Well it wasn't safe with Debbie's parents. Right?

Nancy - No.

David - But would it be safe with Debbie and Lisa, and Mary?

Nancy - Yes.

David - Do you think that maybe you really want and need help from those people, Debbie, Lisa, and Mary?

Nancy - Are you asking me if I think I want them?

David - Yes.

Nancy - Yes.

David - What do you want them to do now?

Nancy - What I want them to do is to help me go break some glass, but they won't.

David - Is there something else you want from them?

Nancy - Maybe.

David - Like when you feel like crying.

Nancy - We are not supposed to ask for help.

David - Is that what Debbie's parents told you?

Nancy - Yes.

David - So you don't have to listen to that anymore do you?

Nancy - I don't know how not to listen.

David - Well if you want help from Debbie, Lisa, Mary, if you want help from them could you just ask them for help? Would that be okay to ask them for help?

Nancy - It's okay to ask them for help?

David - I think so, do you?

Nancy - I don't ask for help.

David - Would you like to ask them for help?

Nancy - I don't like being alone.

David - Would you like to ask them to be with you?

(long silence)

David - Yes? Okay. Could you ask them to be with you now?

Nancy - They're with me.

David - Is it good to have them with you?

Nancy - What do you mean, good?

David - How does it feel?

Nancy - I don't feel like I have to be so tough.

David - You don't have to be so tough. So you can be softer with them.

Nancy - They are being soft.

David - They're being soft, they are being gentle with you. So do you feel like they like you and want to be with you too?

Nancy - (nod)

David - Good.

Nancy - Nobody told them they had to be with me.

David - Nobody told them they had to, they want to be. So do you like being wanted?

(long silence)

David - What's happening now?

Nancy - She's holding me close.

David - She is holding you close? Do you like that?

Nancy - I don't remember anyone doing that before.

David - This is something new.

Nancy - It doesn't hurt.

David - It doesn't hurt?

Nancy - It is sad but it doesn't hurt.

David - So it feels safe so it's not hurting you? It's safe to be sad?

(long silence)

Client - (breathing deeply) (name unknown).

David - What's happening now?

Annie - (soft, child like voice) I just feel so little.

David - You feel so little?

Annie - And so scared.

David - And so scared? Who are you now?

Annie - (crying) I'm Annie.

David - Annie?

Annie - Yes.

David - Is anybody there with you?

Annie - Un-uhm

David - Who's there with you?

Annie - Mary.

David - Mary?

Annie - (crying)

David - Is she holding you or comforting you?

Annie - un-uhm

David - Does it feel good to be with her?

Annie - (crying) I'm sad.

David - Sad.

Annie - (crying)

David - Do you know what you're sad about?

Annie - I don't know. My head hurts a lot, and I like to play and wasn't allowed to.

David - You weren't allowed to play?

Annie - Not before.

David - Debbie's parents wouldn't let you play?

Annie - But I wasn't supposed to tell anybody.

David - You weren't supposed to tell anybody what?

Annie - I can't tell you.

David - Who says you can't tell me?

Annie - My head hurts when I tell anybody and it hurts really bad right now.

David - It's hurting really bad right now? Do you trust Mary? Do you like her?

Annie - I wish she was my mommy.

David - You wish she was your mommy? Maybe you could ask her if you should tell me or not...if it would be good for you or not to tell.

Annie - (crying, soft childlike voice) She says that it is okay to tell, but every time I try to my head hurts bad.

David - Ask her if there is something she can do to help you so you can tell and it won't hurt your head so bad.

Annie - she tells me that my head is going to hurt because I learned to have it hurt because every time I told anybody anything I got hit in the head. That's why it's going to hurt.

David - But this time no one is going to hit you in the head.

Annie - No they won't.

David - So maybe you can say something and your head won't hurt this time.

Annie - When I say that I like to play my head doesn't hurt.

David - That's good. So would it be okay to play now. Ask Mary if now you can play.

Annie - I always have to pretend that I play.

David - You always had to pretend that you played. Now can you really play?

Annie - I can play with Mary in the light.

David - And that's fun, right?

Annie - But I had to tell stories and lie to people and I don't like that.

David - So would you rather tell the truth?

Annie - It hurts when I do that.

David - Because you get hit in the head? Would you like to be able to tell the truth now without getting hit in the head?

Annie - affirmative gesture)

David - Okay, ask Mary if it will be safe now for you to tell the truth now and no one will hit you in the head.

Annie - (affirmative gesture)

David - She said yes?

Annie - Yes.

David - Okay, go ahead and tell me the truth and I won't hit you.

Annie - Mommy, if she thought we were playing too loud or too long she would put us in our room and lock us in there. And if we were loud in our room then she would lock us outside. We had to stay out all day. But we were not to tell anybody because Mommy is a good mommy and she doesn't do that.

David - Now, are you telling me...

Annie - My head hurts.

David - Does your head hurt?

Annie - Yes.

David - Is someone hitting you?

Annie - No.

David - So it is just the fear of someone hitting you?

Annie - Mary says I learned to have my head hurt.

David - She says you learned to have your head hurt. So can you learn to stop having your head hurt?

(long silence)

Annie - Mommy lied a lot.

David - Can you say that a little louder, I didn't hear you.

Annie - Mommy lied a lot.

David - Mommy lied a lot?

Annie - She lied a lot.

David - She really lied a lot.

Annie - She was really mean too.

David - She was mean too?

Annie - I didn't like her.

David - You didn't like her.

Annie - But we're supposed to like Mommy.

David - You're supposed to like her but you really don't?

Annie - No, I don't like her. But I can't tell anyone that.

David - But now it's okay?

Annie - She didn't like Grandma knowing, either. She knew Grandma believed me, so that's why she said I couldn't see Grandma.

David - So you were really badly hurt by your mother?

Annie - What?

David - You've been badly hurt by your mother, her locking you out and lying, and not letting you tell and it has hurt you.

Annie - I don't know what you mean.

David - Did you feel bad about it, did you feel sad?

Annie - I feel bad because I'm not supposed to be mad at her, I'm supposed to like her.

David - You're supposed to like her but really you're mad at her and don't like her. So...

Annie - Sometimes I think she was like, like uh, the witch on the Wizard of Oz. That's who she reminds me of.

David - She was like the witch?

Annie - But that's not nice to say.

David - So ask Mary if it's okay for you to be feeling this way.

Annie - My head doesn't hurt so bad.

David - It doesn't?

Annie - It hurts just a little bit.

David - What are you feeling now?

Annie - Just scary.

David - You're scared? What are you scared of?

Annie - Scared Mommy's coming.

David - You're scared Mommy's coming?

Annie - Because I heard her belt.

David - You heard her belt when she hits you? Is Mary still there with you?

Annie - Yes.

David - Ask Mary if Mommy's coming.

Annie - No, she says she's not.

David - So really, it's safe.

Annie - I thought I heard Mommy.

David - But it wasn't really her.

Annie - No.

David - Maybe it was just the sound of the tape recorder clicking.

Annie - Tape...what?

David - There is a tape recorder recording what you are saying and it just made a click.

Annie - What's that?

David - It's a machine that records your voice so you can later hear what you said.

Annie - Kind of like a record?

David - Yeah, like a record.

Annie - Okay, I'm going to be on it?

David - Well you will be able to hear how you sound. Isn't that neat, you made your own record.

Annie - Can I listen to it?

David - Yeah. When we're finished talking you can take the tape home with you and listen to it. you can do it whenever you want.

Annie - Okay.

David - You're happy with Mary, right? You like being with her?

Annie - She's safe. She's warm.

David - How about someone else? Debbie, and Lisa?

Annie - They're with Nancy.

David - They're with Nancy. Do you want to be with them too?

Annie - I don't think Nancy's as mean as she likes to be.

David - Are you afraid of Nancy? Is she mean?

Annie - No, I'm not afraid of her.

David - Has she ever been mean to you?

Annie - No, I don't think she's as mean as she wants people to think she is. She's not as mean as she'd like to be.

David - You really like her; you think she's pretty nice, actually?

Annie - Yeah.

David - Well that's good. So, do you think you would like to be friends with Debbie and Lisa and Nancy, and play with them, and be in the light with them?

Annie - Yeah, I always like going to the light.

David - That's good. So, do you want to go to the light now and follow them?

Annie - (sound made seems to be affirmative)

David - Good. So, are you with them now?

Annie - Yes.

David - So how's that?

Annie - It feels so good.

David - Good.

Annie - I don't ever want it to go away.

David - Do you want to stay with them?

Annie - Yeah, I do.

David - Do they all want to stay together too?

Annie - Nancy's feeling better.

David - Good. What's happening now?

Annie - There's a lot of talking.

David - Who's talking?

Annie - Debbie and the Guidance, and Mary. I don't know what they're saying.

David - Are they talking...?

Annie - Sounds funny.

David - Are they talking about things that you are too little to understand?

Annie - What do you mean?

David - You can't understand what they are talking about.

Annie - Words are too hard.

David - What do you hear?

Annie - Sounds funny listening, though.

David - It sounds like they're talking about something good? Something that's going to help you?

Annie - No. Because sometimes they are still crying.

David - Who's crying?

Annie - Nancy. It makes me sad to see her cry.

David - Do you want to tell her that?

Annie - I did. I told her. Debbie taught me how to talk quiet.

David - What's happening now?

Annie - I'm listening to all the funny words. I'm going to go to sleep for awhile. I'm tired.

David - So you want to go to sleep, and maybe Debbie will talk to me.

Annie - Yeah, I'm tired.

David - So do you want to go to sleep now?

Annie - Yeah.

David - Do you feel safe sleeping now?

Annie - You're always safe in the light.

David - Good. So you want to go to sleep now.

.Annie - (silence)

David - Okay, go to sleep. (long silence) Debbie, are you there?

Debbie - (soft, adult female voice)Yes.

David - So you are there in the light with Mary and Nancy, Lisa and Annie? Have you been talking to the Guidance?

Debbie - Yes.

David - Do you know what needs to happen now to be able to bring everybody back together?

Debbie - Nancy needs something.

David - What does Nancy need?

Debbie - She needs to go into the very center (audible sighs), the very, very center.

David - The very, very center of the light?

Debbie - Yes.

David - So can you and Mary and everybody take her there now?

Debbie - Most everybody.

David - Ask the Guidance if it would be good for her to go there now with almost everybody.

Debbie - Yes, it is.

David - Take her there now. (long silence) What's happening now?

Debbie - She doesn't want to go.

David - She doesn't want to go?

Debbie - I'm not forcing her. I am trying to encourage her (sighs).

David - Does the Guidance know how you can encourage her to go?

Nancy - (voice changes) What's in the very center?

David - Are you Nancy?

Nancy - Yes.

David - Are they wanting you to go into the very center of the light?

Nancy - Yes.

David - Is Mary there? Can you ask her what is in the very center of the light?

Nancy - She tells me just more of what is with us now.

David - What is with you now?

Nancy - She doesn't give very clear answers.

David - Well, you're in the light now, not the very center, but in the light?

Nancy - Yes.

David - Is there something in the light that is better than not being in the light? Is there something safe or comforting or healing that is good about being in the light?

Nancy - It's warm and if feels so safe.

David - And so...

Nancy - so bright.

David - So the center of the light will be brighter, warmer, and safer. Is that what she's telling you?

Nancy - But I felt so sad when I came this far. Is there going to be more sadness in there?

David - Ask Mary about the sadness. Ask her if it's okay to be sad. Is that going to help you in some way?

Nancy - She tells me that the very center is where the deepest joy and the deepest pain both are...that it's where the two come together for healing.

David - So do you feel like you want healing right now?

Nancy - I don't know if I know what healing is. A lot of what they say does not make sense.

David - So ask Mary if she can tell you something that can clarify it for you.

Nancy - I wish I had Grandma to talk to about it.

David - You wish you could talk to your grandmother?

Nancy - Yes.

David - Is there some way to do that?

Nancy - She's dead.

David - She's dead?

Nancy - (crying) I didn't get a chance to say good-bye.

David - You didn't get to say good-bye.

Nancy - (crying) I couldn't go.

David - So that makes you very sad. Is that what you're so sad about, missing your grandmother?

Nancy - (crying) Nobody would let me go.

David - They wouldn't let you go when you wanted to so badly?

Nancy - (crying) They told me children don't go to funerals. But they told me because I didn't go to see her and that is why she got sick and died.

David - They blamed it on you?

Nancy - (crying and moaning) Oh...oh...

David - That really hurts. What's happening now?

Nancy - (crying) My head hurts. Oh, God, my head hurts. I want it to stop hurting.

David - Ask Mary what has to happen to stop your head from hurting.

Nancy - (crying) Oh!

David - What has to happen to make your head stop hurting?

Nancy - (crying) I don't know, it hurts so bad.

David - Can you ask Mary what will make your head stop hurting?

Nancy - (crying) I can see myself standing at the steps and the telephone and they are telling me Grandma's sick and she's dying. Nancy - (crying) My head...oh...

David - What's happening now.

Nancy - (crying) I just want to cry, I didn't get to go.

David - That's really sad.

Nancy - And I didn't kill her.

David - No.

Nancy - I didn't but they told me I did.

David - They lied to you. I'm, glad you realize you didn't kill her. Do you need some healing for the grief from the loss of your grandmother?

David - It really hurts.

Nancy - Grandma was the only one who did nice things to me.

David - She was the only one who was good to you. You really miss her.

Nancy - She told me that I would grow up to be a good girl.

David - She was right.

Nancy - (sobbing for a long time) I don't like to think about her because I cry when I do.

David - Do you want to feel better?

Nancy - (crying) I want to feel better but I don't know if I can.

David - Ask Mary if you can feel better.

Nancy - She said I can.

David - Ask her what you can do to feel better.

Nancy - (crying) She tells me to hold Annie because she's like Grandma.

David - Can you hold Annie?

Nancy - (crying) Grandma's name was Ann. (sobbing).

David - What's it like holding Annie?

Nancy - (crying) I remember Grandma used to hold me. Oh...I used to sit in her lap and my head would lay against her chest and she would wrap arms around me and just hold me, and tell me that I was going to grow into a special girl.

David - She was right.

Nancy - (crying)

David - What's happening now?

Nancy - (crying) I just told Mary I could go into the light.

David - So you're going into the light now, into the center?

Nancy - (crying) Yes. It's all lies. I didn't do anything to Grandma.

David - No.

Nancy - (crying) It's all lies.

David - That's right.

Nancy - (crying and loud, loud sigh)

David - Are you in the center of the light now?

Nancy - (crying) No.

David - Are you moving towards it?

Nancy - (crying) I don't know if I want to go any further.

David - Do you think you have gone far enough for now?

Nancy - (crying) They tell me to go all the way. It's so hard to, though.

David - Call Mary and Debbie. Can they help make it easier?

Nancy - Yes.

David - Good. What's happening now?

Nancy - I am just moving into the light more. It feels so far away but it's not.

David - It feels far away but really it's pretty close?

Nancy - No. (long sign and sniffling) May I have a tissue?

David - Okay.

Nancy - (crying) Oh.

David - What's happening now?

Nancy - I keep hearing...I keep seeing myself on the top and I keep hearing them tell me that and I just wanted to scream because the only person who ever said they loved me was dying. Oh...(sobbing).

David - It hurts deep.

Nancy - (crying and sobbing) And keep saying it again and I felt like I was all alone. Oh...(sobbing) I just went and hid. The only thing I could do was hide. I couldn't let them see me cry. (whispering) I don't know when she died.

David - So what do you want right now?

Nancy - (crying) I want to know that everything she told me was the truth and that it wasn't lies.

David - That she really loved you?

Nancy - (crying) Yes.

David - You really are growing up to be a good girl?

Nancy - Yes. I was told I would never be a good girl.

David - Ask Mary, you trust Mary, ask Mary, what does Mary say? Did Grandma really love you?

Nancy - (crying) She tells me that Grandma loved me almost as much as she does.

David - That's a lot. Ask her if she thinks you have grown up to be a good girl.

Nancy - (crying) She said yes.

David - Good.

Nancy - (crying and sobbing) Oh...I don't want to cry.

David - Ask Mary what you can do to stop crying.

Nancy - (crying) Come all the way with her.

David - Do you want to go all the way with her now?

Nancy - (crying) Yes.

David - All right. Go all the way with her now.

long silence)

David - What's happening now?

Nancy - (crying) I see why I'm so mad. Oh, I don't know how to go all the way.

David - Excuse me, I didn't hear what you said.

Nancy - (crying) I don't know how to go all the way.

David - You don't know how to go all the way?

Nancy - (sniffling) No.

David - Ask Mary if you can go all the way now.

Nancy - She said yes, she said I know how.

David - Can you just go all the way now? You do know how?

Nancy - (very, very faint whispers)

(long silence)

Nancy - (faintly) It feels so good. (louder) It feels so good.

David - It feels good. So are you in the center now?

Nancy - I feel like I am wrapped up so warm and safe.

David - Good.

Nancy - So much love. It hurts so much too.

David - So you can feel all the love and all the joy and all the pain?

Nancy - (sniffling) Yeah. But I understand now why.

David - You understand why?

Nancy - Why we became so afraid. Why we ran away from each other again.

David - Why did you run away from each other again?

Nancy - (crying) Because Debbie didn't know if Pat was okay and then it reminded me of Grandma.

David - Losing Pat would really be like losing Grandma, somebody who said they loved you.

Nancy - (crying) No. Debbie was on the phone.

David - The fact that she was on the phone reminded you?

Nancy - She heard EMS say that Heather was in the hospital, but they didn't tell her about Pat.

David - But you could not talk to them and that was like you couldn't talk to Grandma.

Nancy - No. When we went to the hospital I had to take it for her because I did not want her to go through the pain (sobbing). But Pat's okay, he's going to be okay.

David - Good. So now that you can understand all of that, is it okay for you all to be together again?

Nancy - Yes. Yes.

David - Good, what needs to happen now for all of you to come together again?

Nancy - Everybody is drawing together, everyone is coming together.

David - Is everyone there?

Nancy - Yes.

David - Good. Can they all come together now?

Nancy - (several deep breaths) Not yet.

David - What needs to happen first?

Nancy - It's a whole new level of understanding has to grow between us all.

David - A new level of understanding has to grow between all of you?

Nancy - Yes.

David - Before you are ready to come together completely?

Nancy - Yes.

David - What needs to happen to create that new level of understanding?

Nancy - Time.

David - Time?

Nancy - I don't feel anything except safe with everyone (sighing).

David - You want to feel safe with everyone?

Nancy - (voice beginning to change) I do feel safe with everyone.

David - You do. Good. Are you still Nancy?

Client - Kind of. Some of us are coming together.

David - Some of you are coming together?

(long silence)

David - What's happening now?

Client - I am aware of two worlds and it's funny.

David - Which two worlds?

Client - I wish I could live in them both...(whispering) but I can't. It feels so good to be there, though.

David - So there is an inner world in the center of the light that you would like to be in?

Client - Yes.

David - But then you also have to live in the outer world. Okay, so before you open your eyes and come back into the outer world, is there anything that needs to happen now to make everything as best as possible to help you move forward in the future towards that better understanding and toward all coming together?

Client - I've been doing that silently.

David - You've been doing that silently?

Client - Yes.

David - Good.

Client - It feels good to have everyone back.

David - It's good to be back with everybody?

Client - Yes.

David - Is there anything else that needs to happen before you open your eyes?

Client - (sighs) We need to pray but I have been doing that.

David - So you need more time to pray?

Client - I think so.

David - Take your time.

Client - (deep breath) So tired.

David - You're tired because you have been through a lot today and you have been through a lot lately.

Client - I'm so tired and I just want to cry, but I don't want to cry.

David - Who are you now?

Client - Debbie.

David - Okay, are you in the light with everybody?

Debbie - Yes. All I want to do is cry. But I don't want to.

David - So you're not sure if you want to cry or not.

Debbie - I do want to but I don't

David - You do but you don't. Can you ask the guidance or Mary if you should cry or not since you do but you don't?

Debbie - Ask them what?

David - Ask them if you should cry or not.

Debbie - When I need to cry I will.

David - Is that what they said?

Debbie - (affirmative gesture)

David - So are you crying now?

Debbie - No.

David - So I guess you don't need to.

Debbie - I have an incredible urge to, though, but I'm not.

David - But when you need to you will, right?

Debbie - Yes.

David - Is there anything else you need to do before you open your eyes?

Debbie - No.

David - So you're ready to end the session now?

Debbie - Yes.

David - Okay.

This is only a portion of a session, to give you an idea of how our sessions went. As you can see, the Holy Spirit is an important force in my life. I believe my spirituality is not only a tool but also a way of life that began long before counseling and continues today.

In the world of MPD/DID experts and therapy, the spiritual helps are frequently referred to as Centers. Are Centers and the Holy Spirit in fact one and the same? I don't know. All I have is the literature and my personal experience with my Guidance, the Holy Spirit.

Throughout scripture and the history of the world, God has assured us of His desire to be with us in our joys, sorrows, doubts, and fears. The New Testament speaks of God's presence when Jesus began His ministry at a wedding feast in Cana; when Jesus healed the blind, the sick, and the lame; when He raised Lazarus from death; when He calmed the water of Galilee; rescued Peter from his fears and doubts while walking on the water; calmed the apostles in the upper room; and when He offered Himself in Thomas' doubts. God was present when the Israelites faced the barriers of the sea, the lack of drinking water and food. As each need was cried out, God answered. Scripture tells us that when Jesus spoke to the disciples of his coming death, he told of another "one" to come, to give comfort and assistance. It is known as the "Comforter," the "Paraclete." John 14: 15-18 teaches, "If you love me and obey the commands I give you, I will ask the Father and he will give you another Paraclete—to be with you always: the Spirit of truth, whom the world cannot accept, since it neither sees him nor recognizes him, but you can recognize him because he remains with you and will be within you. I will not leave you orphaned; I will come back to you." John 14: 26 says, "the Paraclete, the Holy Spirit whom the Father will send in my name will instruct you in everything and remind you of all that I told you." And John 16: 7-14 says, Yet I tell you the sober truth: It is much better for you that I go. If I fail to go, the Paraclete will never come to you, whereas if I go, I will send him to you. When he comes, he will prove the world wrong about sin, about justice, about condemnation.

About sin—in that they refuse to believe in me; about justice—from the fact that I go to the Father and you can see me no more; about condemnation—for the prince of this world has been condemned. I have much more to tell you, but you cannot bear it now. When he comes, however, being the Spirit of truth he will guide you to all truth. He will not speak on his own, but will speak only what he hears, and will announce to you the things to come. In doing this he will give glory to me because he will have received from me, what he will announce to you."

Throughout history people have experienced and written of encounters with the Divine, which always draws them toward wholeness. Much of the world has recognized the experiences of Padre Pio, Theresa of Avila, John of the Cross, and Hildegard of Bingen. Today the world acknowledges the work of Pope John Paul II and Mother Theresa. Evangelists are spreading stories of people who have witnessed God's help and presence. Today we have apparitions occurring at Medjugorje as well as the apparitions of the past such as Lourdes, Fatima, and Guadaloupe. Finally, we have helping professionals such as Bass, LaShan, Rossi, Dossey, and Seigel, to name a few, telling us to incorporate spiritual principles in our health care system because spiritual assistance is available, needed, and a vital part of each individual. In the Courage to Heal, Ellen Bass and Laura Davis wrote about getting in touch with our spiritual part so that we have the needed help to calm down and to become centered or grounded.

Dr. Marion Bilich and Rev. Stephen Carlson wrote in their article, "Therapists and Clergy Working Together: Linking the Psychological with the Spiritual in the Treatment of MPD," that they used the symbols and imagery found in Psalm 23 to help a client create a safe place to work from.

I have seen therapists use their clients' spirituality to help them see their goals more clearly. Those clients have found new hope, have become assertive, and have found a love for themselves that was buried long ago. As I watched David's work with me, I began to understand the concept of using resources available to both the client and the therapist in such a way that the resultant healing is in the core of the client and emanates outward, totally permeating the client, which results in lasting changes.

According to Frank Ochberg, healers known as shamans or medicine men have existed since long before psychiatry came into existence. Their methods of healing always included "a sacred, ritual dimension...The medicine man invoked spiritual assistance...Prayers were said individually and collectively...clinicians must evaluate their client's spiritual potential...their ability to benefit from their own beliefs,...."

David had freedom to follow our lead and use our creativity to facilitate healing. Using a person-centered approach to counseling allowed him to incorporate the positive experiences I had in my spirituality.

In 1993 David and Lee asked permission to use our case in a psychological workshop. They were to be speakers on creativity in counseling. We granted permission, provided David video tape that portion of the talk for us to review. I remember thinking how much we must have grown in trusting the two of them, for us to grant that kind of permission. It required courage and trust from all of my alters to give permission for David and Lee to discuss us and to use our artwork (one piece of which was a self-portrait) in their presentation. During their talk, both David and Lee mentioned that the Holy Spirit always seemed to know exactly what needed to be done; that when the alters listened and did as the Holy Spirit directed, therapy seemed to go smoother; that what the Holy Spirit told us to do always worked. In a lecture given in 1985 Christine Comstock commented that the Centers are the most appropriate resource to use in working with MPD clients because the Center knows the client, the personalities, and the client's history. She further said that it is important to get the client communicating with his or her Center, or spiritual source, that doing so makes healing easier on all parties concerned.

What is the Center? According to Turtle, it had a guidance; an inner voice or sense that directed and guided it if it chose to listen. Like me, Turtle referred to the guidance as the Holy Spirit.

From it we learned what we were never taught: how to best help ourselves. According to Bryant et.al. and Comstock, Centers are Inner Self Helpers (ISH) that lay within each multiple personality. These ISH desire wholeness and healing. They lead the client from within if they are allowed to. They have also been referred to as Centers, Guidance, The Holy One, The Wise One, and the Spirit of Christ within. Based on her experience, Comstock thinks that Centers have a close relationship or a oneness with God. My own belief is that all people possess this inner guide or Center, not just individuals diagnosed with DID.

Bass and Davis think a force exists inside people that searches for healing, growth, and wholeness. They call this force spirituality and say that we need to learn to trust this force so that healing can occur.

Most people in life, not just those with DID, need to learn to trust their inner voice. I think we have buried our internal guidance because our western culture scoffs and ridicules it. Centers offer strength to lean on, comfort and solace. At times I did not want to hear what the Holy Spirit had to say. Fortunately for me, the alter system could not ignore the Holy Spirit for long because the alters found nurturance in the peace and gentleness in its strong and stable presence. Even though I do not always want to hear what the Holy Spirit has to say, I, like my system before integration, cannot ignore it for long. The alters have grown to accept the affirmations given by Mary and the Holy Spirit. They have begun thriving in the gentle strength of the Spirit. In the exquisite pleasure of being accepted by Mary and Holy Spirit, we have learned to give to ourselves what we give to others: love, gentleness, graciousness, and acceptance.

Comstock spoke of a client's experiencing "an overwhelming sense of peace flowing throughout" herself when she began listening to her Center. It seems that the greatest messages Centers give is this: It's okay to make mistakes; you don't have to be perfect, and you are loved just as you are.

While my system enjoyed being with the Holy Spirit, we also tried to get away when confronted. The Holy Spirit seemed to challenge the beliefs held by the alters to protect the system, and asked what could be done about those beliefs. Sometimes the Holy Spirit appeared to hold up a mirror for us—not a mirror showing us our faults, but a mirror of healthy qualities such as a willingness to work, gentleness, devotion, protectiveness, and innocence. Comstock suggests that Centers encourage, support, guide, challenge, point out aspects of people or situations, suggest thoughts and help in any way they can...Usually [Centers] come for one of three purposes: 1) To inform the person of some aspect of life the person had not known, 2) To educate the person about some lesson the person had learned incorrectly, and 3) To complete a situation...."

The Holy Spirit instructed me in all three of these areas. It helped me learn what I was never taught or exposed to in my immediate family: patience, gentleness, kindness, and respect. The Holy Spirit re-educated me as to what self-worth and self-value are. It helped me search the contradictions in my life to find the truth and then apply that truth in my life. The Holy Spirit supported me as we walked up to memories and experiences, traveled through what I previously had denied and repressed, and I exited a little wiser, freer, and more peaceful.

We began responding quickly and willingly to David's continual encouragement to allow the Holy Spirit to direct our healing journey. Most of the sessions were conducted with David asking the alter in control to ask the Guidance what needed to happen, how to go about something, or what was needed. The Holy Spirit always responded. Sometimes the response was as simple as "allow Mary to lead you." A couple times it told me to "follow David's lead; he knows." Whenever the Holy Spirit responded by telling me to follow David's lead, it was usually because the controlling alter refused to tell David what it understood the Holy Spirit to have said. When David led without being told what the Holy Spirit said, he would do or say what the Spirit had previously directed. When David led without being told what the Holy Spirit said, he did what the alter had been told to do. I think and believe that the spirit within me communicated with whatever spirit of faith existed in David. I believe that spirit-to-spirit communication between people is possible and that this is how David was able to accurately guide us through some experiences. I also believe that God tells us through His Spirit what we need to know for a particular situation. I believe God answered my requests, my prayers for direction, strength, courage, wisdom, and guidance in the sessions. I prayed not only for myself but also for David and Lee.

As a therapist, I have experienced a "knowing" I cannot explain. I have experienced the images and sensations reported by my clients. Sometimes I have felt lost when I do not experience what appears to be spirit-to-spirit communication with a client. I expect God to guide and direct me spiritually when I work with my clients. I believe that when I am experiencing this "knowing" I have an obligation to use it and that I would be negligent as a therapist if I did not use this gift of knowledge when it is available. I call this spirit-to-spirit communication or "knowing" a gift because in Christianity this "knowing" is a gift of the Holy Spirit known as a "Word of Knowledge." All forms of spirituality have described an experience of "knowing." If such a free and powerful resource is made available to me to help make a breakthrough when all other techniques and modalities have failed, then I think I have a responsibility to use it.

My system and I enjoyed working with and spending time with the Holy Spirit. We found it safe, loving, and patient. When the alters chose not to acknowledge the Holy Spirit's directions, the Holy Spirit or Mary or both would speak firmly but understandingly to us. The Holy Spirit and Mary never forced any of us to do anything; according to Comstock, this is typical of Centers. She notes that Centers do not push for compliance but, rather, allow alters the freedom to willingly cooperate with the Center. She also notes that sometimes alters are stubborn and refuse to cooperate. The Center then waits for the alter to come around and work with the Center much the way I used to wait for my child when she was intrigued by something she had never seen.

I have not understood the use of the word Center for the one inside who guides us; I only know that one exists within me who cries with me, laughs with me, and listens to me. This one helps me find out how to get better, how to be the person I was born to be. If others want to call it a Center or Inner Self-Helper, I guess they can, but for me, this one is the Holy Spirit.

Prayer is a part of spirituality and my spiritual life. It is my life. I have said that I prayed for wisdom, direction, and guidance for both David and myself, that I prayed about putting my ritual together and about how to change my life. My method of praying may be familiar to some, unfamiliar to others. Initially I chose a location away from my home at 8 a.m. where I could pray uninterrupted. I would sit in silence, asking God to bring me into His presence. Sometimes I would speak silently to Him, asking Him questions. Other times I simply meditated, centering myself on God, Jesus, or the Holy Spirit. I usually kept paper and pencil with me so I could write down my questions and any thoughts, feelings, or understandings I experienced. I kept these notes in my journals where I could reflect on them periodically and talk about them with my spiritual director.

Most of my prayer was in a prayer language. A prayer language is prayer spoken in a language other than one's native tongue. Romans 8:26 and 27 supports this phenomenon: "The Spirit too helps us in our weakness, for we do not know how to pray as we ought; but the Spirit himself makes intercession for us with groanings that cannot be expressed in speech. He who searches hearts knows what the Spirit means, for the Spirit intercedes for the saints as God himself wills." This was and still is a very personal, private form of prayer, which I guard carefully. My prayer language is a communication between God and me, between the Holy Spirit and each alter. It is directed by the Holy Spirit, who intercedes on my behalf when I do not know what or how to pray.

I used my prayer language not only in private prayer time but also during my sessions with David. This language enabled us to express ourselves when we lacked an adequate vocabulary. When David suggested I ask the Holy Spirit something, I would do so silently, in my prayer language. I was careful never to let myself speak these prayers out loud. One day while our session was being taped, I was very quiet, silently conversing with the Holy Spirit in my prayer language. David asked me what was happening. The alter David was working with answered him, but it answered him in the prayer language before I or any other alter could stop it. I had previously understood from the Holy Spirit that it would be safe to allow David to know of this form of prayer, that he would respect it. Although I knew the Holy Spirit would not mislead us, I and several alters refused to allow David knowledge of this style of conversation in our life. We still feared David would have us hospitalized. Finally, one alter decided to trust David to honor the language, and allowed him to hear it. David asked me about my prayer language and encouraged me to share it with him. I did this by explaining that every time he would tell me to ask the Holy

Spirit's advice or opinion, I would speak in this way. My responses to David would be what I understood to be responses from the Holy Spirit. When I shared with David the conversations between the Holy Spirit and myself, I identified them as thoughts, words and understandings that I sensed rather than heard. I knew no other way to identify them.

In his person-centered approach David recognized the power this form of prayer had in my life. He also saw it as a positive resource for us and began encouraging me and my alters to use it openly in sessions. I thought about David's suggestion to use it in therapy and decided that since he had already heard it, I had nothing to lose.

I began using it in my counseling visits with him. From then on my prayer language became a conscious part of our work. I had to remind myself several times that this form of communication with God is a gift given from God for our use before I began feeling safe using it in counseling.

Even though at times I became angry with David for prodding and challenging me to use my spirituality, I respect him and thank him. If I had to repeat the entire process, I would want him to handle things exactly as he did. His respect for my gifts as well as his encouragement to use them gave me permission to respect myself and accept the gifts God had given me. David's acceptance and encouragement to use the resources I had made it easier for my mentally and emotionally stubborn feet to continue walking the path they needed to follow in order to heal.

I finally began to believe and accept the reality that I no longer had to hide who I was. I no longer had to deny gifts of healing for myself. Here were two professionals (David and Lee) who did not believe as I believed, yet they accepted what I believed and what I (until now) would not accept. It is wonderful that God would use someone holding different beliefs to help me free my own. I am thankful I did not follow the advice of acquaintances within my church who cautioned me not to use David's and Lee's skills. I chose to listen to what the Holy Spirit was saying and continued working with David and Lee. God's Spirit assured me that my work with these two therapists would open not only my eyes and heart but also theirs to something God had for everyone. I have no doubt that David and Lee learned from our work together as much as I did.

Even though I sometimes thought David was prying where he had no right to be (for example, in my prayer language), I recognized it as an important therapeutic strategy that would keep me moving toward healing. I am not sure how often other therapists use something such as a client's prayer language or belief in the Holy Spirit in counseling, but I believe the truly astute and wise therapist will press beyond his or her own beliefs, knowledge, fears, and inhibitions to seek out this spiritual helper and use it in the therapy session.

Therapists will always be challenged to use whatever is healthy in the client. Not only do therapists need to be willing to use their clients' spirituality, but they also need to be willing to use their own spiritual awareness to connect with that of their clients'. It may be difficult to share such a deep part of oneself, but good comes from doing so. Therapists can experience fewer episodes of feeling "stuck" when they call on God for help.

In More Than One, Dr. Terri Clark writes, "Those of us on the treatment team do not use only the tools we learned in schools or the ideas we get out of journals: we call on God to assist us with His divine power to remove the barriers to reintegration. Fortunately for all of us, a real and loving God will help those who need help and help those who provide help."

God does and will help all who ask for His help. Individuals need to be daringly introspective when going through therapy if they are to experience healing and integration and achieve personal growth, both spiritually and psychologically. That means they need a courage that only God can provide. It is not easy to make this inward journey; it is often painful and many resist it. But how else will we truly know who we are? For the one diagnosed with DID, the journey inside has already begun. This is exactly where I found myself as each alter acquired the courage to make such a journey to put ourselves back together.

NOTES

NOTES

Chapter Four
Techniques and Tools

I have described various therapeutic tools that were used in my healing work, such as hypnosis, spiritual guidance, video-taped sessions, and dream work. Other tools we used were being honest in therapy, mapping my internal world, painting, analyzing dreams, keeping a journal, researching the literature, adding a co-therapist, speaking to relatives, applying logic and reasoning, and using family therapy.

Honesty

Honesty must exist for a therapeutic relationship to work. I wanted to refuse to tell David—or David and Lee together—instructions I was receiving from my spiritual guide, and at times I did omit parts of what I understood. I should have been honest about everything I was being told. I also needed to be honest about my having become conditioned to a particular chair. I eventually told David that my sitting on the sofa was a refusal to work and a maneuver to control the session, to maintain the "status quo," to keep David "in the dark." Being honest meant that no alter could make up things or "pretend" with David or me. Being honest required that neither I nor any alter would discount or discredit anyone or any other alter. It also meant that I could trust David not to hospitalize me or lock me away, and he could trust me not to hurt myself or attempt suicide.

Mapping

I had already painted the safe place with caves to hide in, but now I needed to try to put into a tangible form what was occurring inside the safe place. David asked me if I could describe my internal world and note where everyone was. I was unable to verbalize what I was learning about myself, so I made a "map" of my world. I drew a new map each time the location and relationships of my alters changed. These maps helped me see which alters were more prone to working together and how all the alters related, or were related, to one another. They also helped me keep everyone sorted out. David found the maps useful in helping him identify alters who clustered together.

Pre Therapy

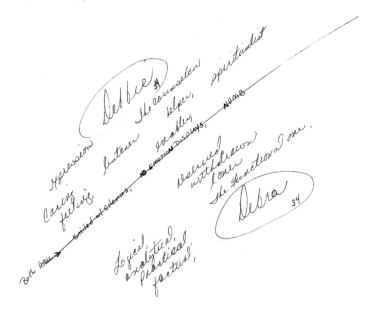

PHASE I - entry into treatment
w/ David

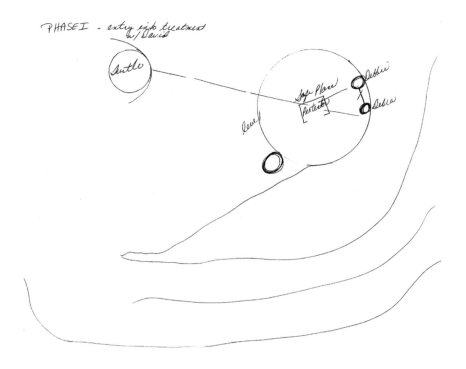

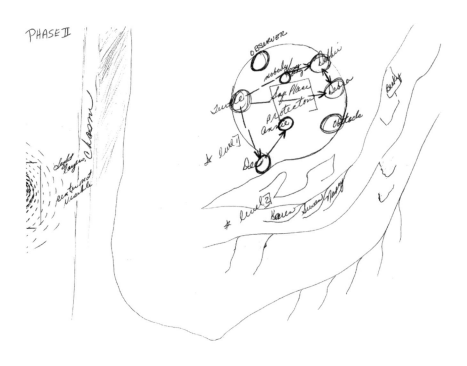

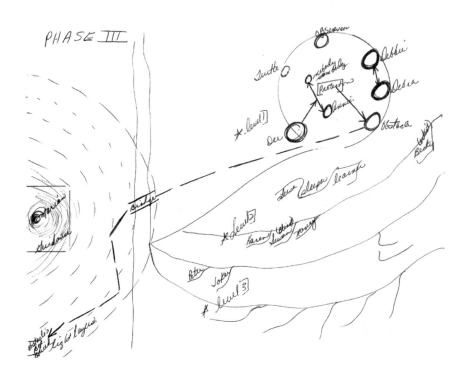

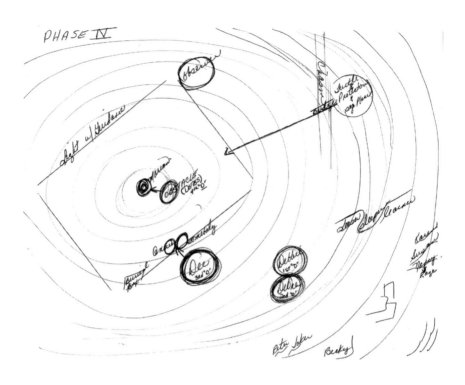

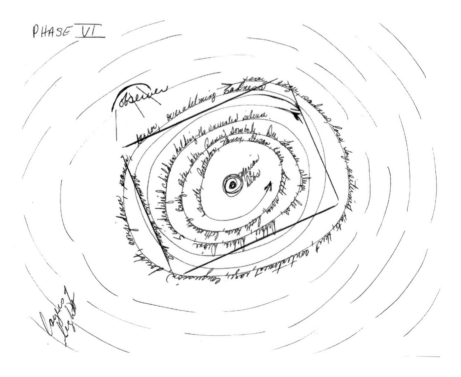

PHASE Ⅵ

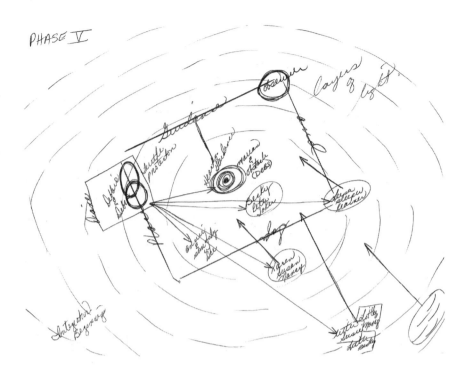

PHASE Ⅶ

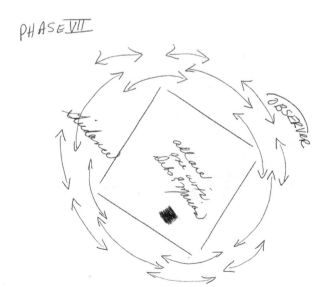

Artwork

I mentioned earlier that Becky was the painter. Our paintings taught me several things about myself. One was that we seldom used more than black, white, and two or three other colors. An example would be black, white, blue, and yellow; or black, white, brown, yellow, and blue. I still follow this scheme, even when decorating and furnishing my home or office. The second thing I learned was that when I studied the various art pieces, I sensed they were presenting messages such as "things are not as they seem," "look beyond the surface," "appearances are deceiving," and "everyone's perception is different."

As I think about this I realize this is true. In everyday life reality is not always as it seems, and most of us walk around living with distorted perceptions. As citizens, whether private or public, we need to always keep God by our side to help us look beyond what we see.

Becky expressed herself through art. She could take any experience she or any other alter was having and transform it into quilts, paintings, drawings, applique pictures, and sculptures. She did not understand the technicalities of space, volume, contrast, and perception, but she knew how to use color and symbols to show our feelings, what we were going through. Our work not only pulled at our emotions, but it also tugged at other people's emotions.

I noted earlier that my art instructor was unable to understand my inability to grasp artistic concepts and to produce quality work consistently. I wanted to be consistent; I also wanted to explain to him that some part of me was the artist, but I felt frustrated and trapped. How could I tell my art instructor that I had called upon a 10-year-old alter named Becky to listen to him explain what was needed in a particular work and then do it. How could I, an adult, a psychology and counseling student, explain Becky to him? I couldn't allow anyone to think there was something wrong with me. I told myself he would never believe me if I did tell him, and even if he did believe, he would never understand.

Just prior to graduation I finally spoke with him about my artist alter. I needed to be honest with him in order to continue helping myself. He surprised me by telling me he had already suspected it a while back, that he had been reading about art therapy and had come across a couple articles about artwork by people diagnosed with MPD. He said that what he had read made him think of me. Apparently, when Becky worked she showed no awareness of anyone or anything, including the instructor. (Becky never acknowledged anyone except David and me.) My instructor said he noticed my lack of awareness during these periods, and that I behaved differently: younger, especially when he explained concepts in terms a young person could grasp. He also noted a significant difference between the work I did when I was myself, as everyone knew me, and the work I did when I seemed younger and ignored him.

As I study my artwork I continue to be struck with awe by the gentleness it contains. Our work prevented me from feeling overwhelmed by my emotions. Whether other people responded the same way, I don't know.

The core personality found safe in divine protection.

Frustration was mounting and the only safe way to express it without hurting myself was in art.

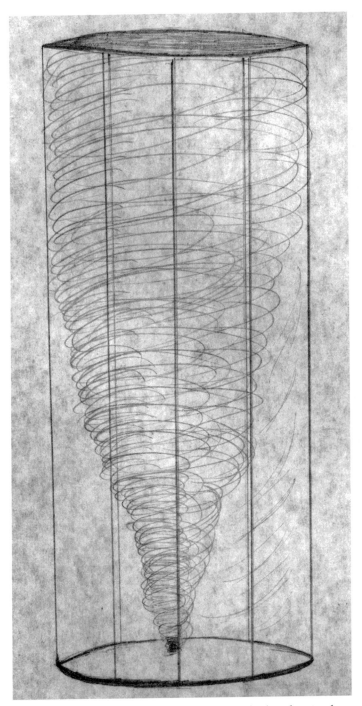

My life felt like it was a raging tornado locked up but in danger of breaking free.

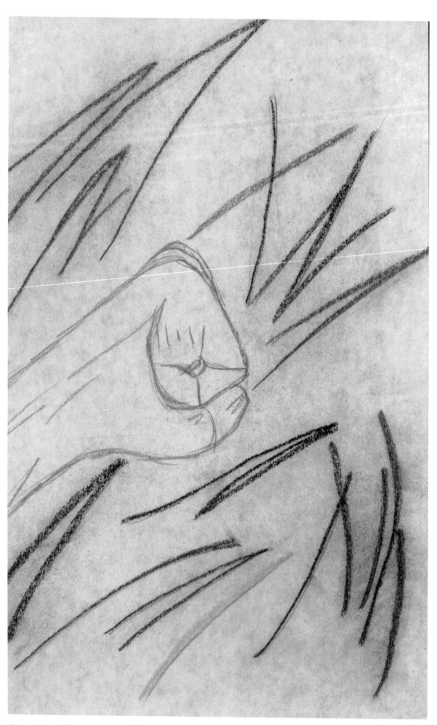

I must not loose control.

Desolation bides the life that exists.

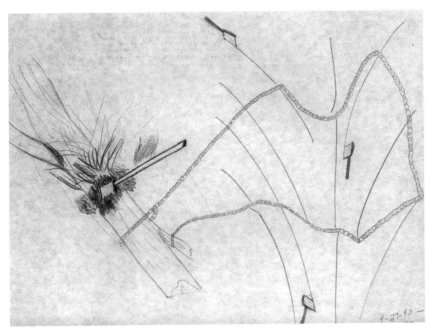

I am trying to hack my way to freedom but I couldn't do it alone.

105

Life is precariously balanced an must be protected

I was making progress as I allowed myself to pass through the doors locking my life away, exposing my past.

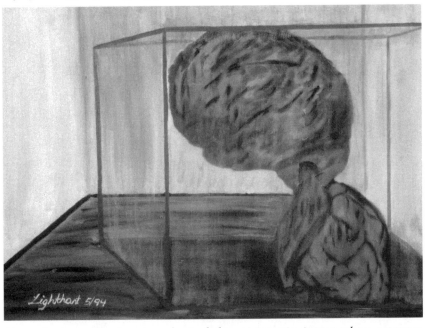

Abuse Isolates *The heart and mind do not remain intact when a person experiences abuse*

107

Dreams

I had numerous dreams during the time we worked with David. Two of those dreams called my attention to areas of denial I was clinging to. In my first dream I held four miniature animals in the palm of my hand. Three became lost while I was walking with them. I looked for them but couldn't find them. I didn't want to lose the fourth animal, which was a turtle, so I put it in a safe place and told it to stay there. The turtle cried at being left alone; it wanted to stay with me.

In the second dream I had a basket full of miniature animals I was supposed to be taking care of. I was out shopping with them one day when I discovered that, one by one, they were disappearing. I retraced my steps but couldn't find them. I looked in the basket, which I had placed in my cart, and found more were missing. I became frightened and frantic. I searched the basket and found a hole in the bottom. I now had only four animals left. I knew they could not survive on their own and I had to keep them safe. I began walking toward the exit when I saw another one fall from the cart. I picked it up and put it back in my basket. When I did, I noticed that one of the other three looked dead. I picked it up and found it was cut in half, although it was not bleeding. I tried to put it back together so it would live, but I couldn't. I began crying and couldn't stop. The dream ended with the animals and me disappearing.

David diagnosed me with MPD after I had these dreams but before I recounted them to him, if I remember correctly. I did not want to accept the diagnosis, but the dreams matched the symptoms I presented in counseling. They also seemed to explain in part the writings I found in my personal journals. As I reflect on them now, I see they were indicating what had happened in my life, that I had lost myself and that some alters had even split apart.

I had other dreams that indicated when I was reverting to old habits. In the first of two repetitive dreams, I owned an old house that was falling apart. People were rummaging through it, taking what they wanted without permission. I would politely try to stop them by taking my things away from them and putting them back in my house, but people kept going in and taking them.

Every time my dream ended this way I would find myself getting stuck in counseling. I would resume denying my experiences, pain, and reality, and I would revert to old coping mechanisms to solve problems. When I stopped and changed what I was doing to help myself, when I stopped denying my life and what was happening in counseling, I would have the same dream but with a different ending. The end of the dream would change from people taking what I kept putting away to my getting angry and renting a truck, loading my belongings into it, retrieving things people were stealing from me, putting those things in the truck and driving away. People would stare after me with shocked looks on their faces. After the dream ended like this, I would learn more about myself and my life; I would feel increased self-respect and confidence.

The other repetitive dream helped me understand I was running and hiding to protect myself. In this dream I had a big, beautiful house on a cliff overlooking the cean. I lived there with my husband and a foster child. We wanted to adopt the child, and went through the necessary steps. One day a couple of caseworkers came to interview me. They talked with me, then said I could not keep the child. They tried to take the child from me, but I grabbed her and ran into a room, slipping through a secret opening in a wall that led to a hidden passage. The house was full of hidden passages that eventually led to the beach. I hid in the passages, but the caseworkers found the secret opening and pursued us. Still holding the child, I reached the beach safely while the caseworkers, having lost me, had to retrace their steps into the house.

This dream stopped repeating itself when I accepted the diagnosis of MPD and worked with it instead of denying it. This dream ended with the caseworkers eventually finding their way through the passages to the beach and allowing me to keep the child.

In another dream I had, a shadowy figure I couldn't identify was holding a small gift-wrapped box in the palm of one of his hands. He was pulling things out of it. I got angry and told the person to stop, that the box was mine and no one else's business. The shadow put everything back, replaced the lid, and offered the box to me. As soon as I took it, the box grew so that I had to hold it with both hands. I set the box down and opened it. I looked inside and saw things from my life, the things I had lost a long time ago. I understood this dream to be the therapeutic relationship I had with David. My dreams were telling me how I was doing. They were becoming my friends instead of my tormentors.

Journaling

One way I helped myself overcome my past was to journal. I approached journaling two ways: writing spontaneously in personal journals, and using workbooks and reading published writing journals. Personal journals were made up of ruled loose leaf paper in 3-ring binders. In my personal journals I recorded my frustrations, memories, dreams, high points, low points, the process and progress of my counseling work. These journals provided an account of my journey and a history to look back on for encouragement. Published writing journals used were: The Courage to Heal Workbook, A Garden in the Snow Mountains Journal, and Managing Ourselves Journal. These journals presented ideas and questions that gave me a directed search for my inner recesses and a directed evaluation of what I was learning and what was happening to me.

Education

Another useful therapeutic tool was education, gained by researching the available literature. I resisted reviewing the literature initially, but when I gave in and researched existing literature on MPD, I found answers and explanations for my experiences, questions, and frustrations. These answers helped me accept the reality of my experiences and helped me continue working with David to achieve my goals.

I had two reasons for not wanting to read available literature. First, I did not believe in MPD. Two, I did not want to be given suggestions of behaviors that I might unconsciously incorporate into my behaviors.

Co-Therapist

David and I used a co-therapist, Lee, in some of our work together. She was not present at every visit but attended sessions at my request or when David and I thought her presence would be beneficial. Lee's presence seemed to be a catalyst for the alters and memories associated with my mother. She brought out those alters who held the stories and interactions between my mom and me.

Desensitization

I used desensitization to dissolve the terror I experienced when anything came near or touched my throat. Since Lee's participation in my sessions acted as a catalyst for the alters, her participation in desensitization was key and pivotal to my healing work. I again invited Lee to participate as co-therapist. David maintained his position as my therapist, probing, challenging, and encouraging me while Lee risked touching my throat. I say "risked" because I had told her stories of my attacking people in the past.

Lee stood behind the chair I sat in and waited until I told her I was ready for her to touch my throat. David acted as a coach, constantly talking to me, telling me to breathe, to relax, to keep Mary and Guidance with me. Reminding me to breathe was critical because when I became scared I would stop breathing (which is typical). I would hold my breath; this enabled me to shut off any emotions and dissociate sooner.

When we first began using desensitization I was unable to tolerate any touch on my throat, so we changed the strategy. Lee continued to stand behind me, but instead of touching my throat she began by touching the side of my neck. This worked, and after a while I was able to tolerate her touch on my neck. Then she began slowly moving her finger closer to my throat. Eventually Lee was able to hold her hands around my neck for a few seconds without my fighting to get free. This exercise was repeated over several sessions. I was learning to stay present and not dissociate. I was learning to let go of my fear. I went from complete intolerance of someone's hands on my throat to an uncomfortable tolerance.

When I was able to both emotionally and mentally survive Lee's hands on my throat without dissociating, David and Lee coached me in pushing the hands away in a safe, assertive manner. I had neither learned nor been able to remove the hands I remembered choking me. They had been much stronger than I, and I had frozen under the look in the eyes behind those hands. I had never been allowed to protect myself. Lee helped unlock the memory behind my terror by being the hands in my memory. To protect herself from harm she stood behind my chair and taught me to protect myself without hurting anyone.

I wanted to desensitize my throat and neck to touch because the sensitivity in my throat had become so strong that I felt as if I were always choking, even when nothing was near my neck. David and Lee used caution and did not push me more than I could tolerate, and I did not attack them. This therapy helped me in many ways: I have not attacked anyone since desensitization; I can wear necklaces, scarves, and clothes against my neck and throat; I no longer pull at the necklines on my clothing; I do not feel as if I am always choking; I enjoy a cat purring at my neck; I can touch my own throat; doctors can touch my throat without my dodging them or tensing my muscles; children can wrap their arms around my neck and hug me; and my husband can kiss my throat and neck. Once in awhile I relive the terror that I am trapped and someone is choking me. When that occurs, I visualize a gentle kitten in my lap. I imagine myself feeling the kitten crawling up to my neck, nudging my chin with its head while it purrs and settles down to sleep. When I do this, my fear dissipates.

Relatives

Talking to relatives was beneficial to my therapy. None of my family members are close, either geographically or emotionally, and I don't know most of my relatives. I needed answers about what had happened, and confirmation or correction of my memories, so in September 1992 I left my comfortable isolation from my family to speak with various siblings and relatives. First I spoke with three of my four brothers.

One of them confirmed pictures I was unable to rid my mind of. I wanted to believe my parents would never beat us, that the pictures in my mind were a result of my overactive imagination. Another brother also remembered some of the pictures I was trying to deny. He provided missing information about a particular beating that one of us had received. For me this memory was a series of flashes that made no sense if I tried to work with them as they were. He filled in some of the blank spots, and I realized these flashes were in reality a memory—one I really wanted to deny. He was able to provide details of our mother chasing one of us with a baseball bat and how she wielded that bat (some of the pictures that were flashing in my mind). I had tried so hard not to remember, but now someone else remembered it too. My brothers confirmed my memories. "My memories are real! I'm not making them up!"

I then spoke with my two youngest brothers. One admitted abuse existed and told how it had affected his life. The other one would only say his life began when he moved away from home. He said he refused to acknowledge the first 18 years of his life, that those years were best forgotten.

After I spoke with my brothers, one of my sisters-in-law

drove me to the town where most of the abuse against me occurred. The purpose was to find the house I had lived in. The town was about two and a half hours away, and the house was eight miles outside the town. When I was a child the house was located in the woods beyond the farms outside of town. I had not been to the town in more than 24 years, and I did not recognize it. Farms still dotted the land surrounding the town, but large neighborhoods had replaced the woods.

My sister-in-law and I finally found the house when I used my ability to "sense the presence" of the place by feeling my way there. I did this by closing my eyes and allowing myself to feel like a young girl between the ages of 7 and 12. I was able to sense the surroundings we were in, the woods I grew up in. I was aware of the vastness of the woods and the tall woodland grasses. I smelled the wild plants. I could hear the birds chirping and the squirrels chattering as I allowed myself to revisit the environment where I had always sought refuge. I felt the presence of my brothers and myself as children. My body began feeling tugs to "head home." I followed the tugs to the right, left, and forward, and we drew closer. I opened my eyes to see the old oak tree we'd stood under waiting for the school bus. All that was left of the tree was a stump, but I could feel us waiting there. I immediately recognized the layout of the land around the tree and its location relative to the surrounding hills and valleys, and I knew I was close. I'd always liked getting on the bus to go to school, and hated getting off the bus after school. At the old bus stop I could feel a tug on the left side of my body, so I directed my sister-in-law to turn left. We slowly drove a few hundred feet when I again felt the tug to turn left.

I looked up and saw the house I remembered. The house was for sale, so I was able to walk around without looking suspicious. I got out of the car for a closer look and saw that it was the same house I'd lived in. I compared the height and size of the house and the location of doors and windows to the picture in my mind. I was conscious of the feeling that I was a bad girl and that I had to stay outside. All of my previous fears and emotions poured over me like floodwaters. The fear was not of being "caught" looking around, it was of being in danger, in trouble. At the same time I was nostalgic for the autumn weather and Halloween, the hayride to town for trick or treating. I allowed myself to look around outside, but I would not go inside. I was afraid the memories would rush back and I would lose control. My sister-in-law encouraged me to go in, but I refused. She had no idea what I was experiencing. I did not think it wise for me to go in and risk another flood of memories when I had no knowledgeable therapeutic support present. She did not know about my DID diagnosis, and I was about 10 hours by air travel from my therapist.

When we returned from seeing the house, one of my brothers took me to visit my parents' house while they were out shopping. He helped me find photos from my childhood. One photo confirmed that the house I had just visited was where I had lived. Another photo provided evidence of the bruises and injuries inflicted on us. As I looked at the pictures, I began to shake. I felt scared and trapped, as if I were bad. I felt as if I were in shock, in a trance. Here I was, holding photographic evidence of the abuse I had suffered—the proof I had told David I wished I had. I rushed out of Mom and Dad's house, terrified they would come home and find me there. How sad that a 38-year-old woman would be terrified of her parents.

I followed up the conversations with my brothers and the visit to the old house by contacting one of my aunts. She told me of things she had seen in my family when she visited us. She told me how she had seen my parents treat us and how they had responded to her when she confronted them about their behaviors. She told me of some of my family's intergenerational abuse. She also suggested I contact a great-great aunt. I wrote to this elderly aunt, and her reply erased all remaining doubts that my family had a history of abuse. Without going into details, my great-great aunt simply stated she had hoped the abuse had finally stopped.

Even though speaking with my relatives was painful, I have never regretted it. They helped me to stop hating myself. Their information helped me see myself as loving instead of hateful and despicable. Their revelations put to rest my doubts about the accuracy of my memories.

Logic and Reasoning

David and I used logic and reasoning to help the different alters investigate, challenge, and correct their thinking, assumptions, and beliefs. We used it to test the validity of our thoughts and beliefs: that if the secrets were told, the beatings would resume; that if we told what happened no one would believe us and we would be locked up.

David had to continually remind the alters that Mom and Dad were not in the room. He had to remind us that these things happened a long time ago and that they would not begin again if we remembered and talked about them. Sometimes I would have to ask an alter to find Mom or Dad at a particular moment. They never found them because David and I always worked with the alters in the present. David often challenged alters to explain why they wouldn't trust the Holy Spirit, Jesus, or Mary when Annie, Nobody/Somebody, Dee and I trusted them. For every excuse an alter gave for not trusting, David or Lee countered with examples where earned trust was already experienced and established. It always came down to the alters making the decision that they either "want to or don't want to" trust (believe, change, help, ask for help). David always seemed to "back the alters into a corner" forcing them to decide whether they were not able to trust something or do something, or just didn't "want to."

Some of the alters did not like this and expressed anger at David in our journals. Gradually the length of time an alter argued or held out with David shortened to mere seconds. Over time they learned they didn't need to prove their point, their individuality, their existence, or their purpose to David, Lee or themselves.

Family Therapy

We practiced family therapy in two ways. One was within my "traditional" family: husband, wife, and children. This involved clarifying rules between parents and children, setting boundaries between husband and wife as well as parents and children, and establishing role expectations of each family member. It also meant investigating how my family of origin was influencing the dynamics in my current family.

The other type of family therapy took place among all of my alters. They each needed individual therapy, but once we accomplished that they still needed to learn how to interact with one another, where their boundaries lay, and what to expect from themselves and one another. They needed to learn how to function and live as one unit, just as a traditional family has to learn. The alters learned, and they became one functioning body.

NOTES

NOTES

NOTES

Chapter Five
Final Ritual and Integration

The Holy Spirit became an integral part of our therapy once David became aware of Its presence and power in my life. When my alter system wanted to integrate, David suggested asking the Holy Spirit if it was time. The Holy Spirit said it was, but also said that this integration would not be permanent. I could not understand why we integrated and then split apart, not once but several times. I would become frustrated and angry; I wanted this finished. I considered each integration and splitting apart as a step backward, as failure to heal. I was impatient with myself. I wanted to integrate. I had to accept that integration eventually would occur and would remain intact, but not until the time was right.

During the first few days of 1995, I understood from the Holy Spirit that we could use a ritual to close the past. I told David, and he assigned me homework, telling me to ask the Guidance how this ritual was to be performed. The Holy Spirit directed me to prepare for the ritual in the following ways:

- Have five other people present: David, two spiritual supporters and two therapists who work with DID.
- Have each person ask me one of the questions of accountability that the Holy Spirit said each alter needed to answer, with David asking the first and last questions.
- Display some of my artwork, to remind us of our accomplishments and symbolize the work we had done.
- Ask David to explain the purpose of the gathering, which was to close the past and open the future.
- Explain to those present their roles and why I had chosen them.
- Select music.

I prepared this outline for the ritual:

Ritual Outline

1. Arrival—Set up anything that needs to be set up.
2. Greet arrivals and thank them for coming.
3. Introductions - Debra: explain purpose and what I hope to accomplish; distribute any handouts. David: briefly what we have been doing up to this point over the years and the process we have used (similar to the New York presentation David and Lee did in 1993).
4. David - Play first musical selection on tape:The Warrior is a Child."
5. David - Acknowledge all of my alters (will leave to David to decide how).
6. David - Helps me (if necessary) to move internally, seeking next steps.

Things I have understood the Holy Spirit saying needed to be addressed (which may be addressed in any order as directed but which need to be addressed):

   a. The work will be done in core of person and in deep center of light.
   b. I will play the music I wrote: a song of healing, surrender, and acceptance.
   c. Group members will ask questions of accountability.
   d. My pastor will direct anointing and laying on of hands at the appropriate time.
   e. I will pray in my prayer language.
   f. David will play the second song on the tape: "A Time for Building Bridges."
   g. David will play final music on tape.
   h. Group members will offer insights, prayers, and impressions.
   i. I will complete the ritual by returning, stabilizing, remembering, and processing.

These are the accountability questions David and the rest of the group asked: David: Will you surrender your secrecy and privacy?

Therapist: Will you surrender your excuses?

David: Will you own your pain, sorrow, anger, grief, and sexuality, and then surrender them to the Holy Spirit?

Pastor: Will you allow the Guidance (Holy Spirit) the freedom to heal you mentally, emotionally, physically, and spiritually as necessary?

Friend: Will you go where the Holy Spirit leads, to love yourself with Its love?

Psychiatrist: Will you forgive those who abused and hurt you? Will you forgive yourself your thoughts and reactions, accepting whatever comes, unknown though it may be?

David: Will you go where the Guidance leads, accepting the gifts it has given you and using these gifts openly where needed?

David and I launched into the ritual using the outline I had prepared. I explained the purpose of everyone's presence and the role each had in this session. David explained what he and I had been working on over the past four and a half years. He explained some of the artwork I had done and how it had helped my system work through our trauma. Then we began the music. The songs used in the ritual held special meaning for me; they spoke to my heart and spirit. They expressed bits of what I was experiencing and expressing throughout my healing walk. These songs were "The Warrior is a Child." by Twila Paris; "A Time For Building Bridges," by Carey Landry; the music to a song I wrote, which I have included in the chapter "Acceptance"; and the theme song from the movie 10 Seconds.

As the ritual began I immediately focused my attention on David, to help me forget about everyone else in the room. Although I felt nervous and distracted, I was still able to move with Mary and the Guidance to the inner place where we always did our work. As we moved with the Holy Spirit into the deep inner core of our being, each of us relaxed in complete safety, peace, and love. The outside world vanished, as did our fear of looking ridiculous before five other people. David proceeded with the outline. As with all of our other sessions, he continually reminded me to ask the Guidance for direction: What needs to happen? How should we do it? Is now the time to move on? What should we do next? Some of the alters still had fears and reservations. Some of them needed to assure themselves that the other people in the room were safe. Dee challenged the safety of the psychiatrist and the others by directly confronting them. David continued as he had in our previous sessions: challenging, probing, and reassuring all within me.

We worked at dissolving any existing doubts and reservations the alters expressed. Then we asked each alter or group of alters to join together and help one another. Current fears surrounding this decision were addressed among David, the Holy Spirit, and my system. The alters acknowledged their commitment to and desire for completeness.

Going into the core of who I was, was like going into the depths of the mountains or woods.

The accountability questions were directed to my entire system. The alters discussed each question at length before answering. Finally they allowed the last of their reservations to fall away, and my entire system came together to answer "yes" to all the questions the Holy Spirit wanted asked of us.

After answering the questions we were invited deeper into the core of who we were. We were familiar with our core; we had been there in our last couple of sessions with David, and we never wanted to leave. This place was protected by a source of energy we had to pass through when going into and coming out of it. Moving through the energy was uncomfortable. We could feel a tremendous strength and power in it, and felt as if we were being jolted by electrical shocks. We moved with the Holy Spirit through the energy and reached the deep inner core. Inside the core was a magnificent peace, joy, acceptance, and welcoming.

David continued with the outline, asking if it was time for Fr. to lay hands on us and anoint us. We understood that now was the time. Fr. anointed us and invited the other people present to join him in laying hands on us and praying. When they did, an unexpected event took place: integration occurred. Neither David nor I had been warned that this might happen and I had no expectation for integration to occur.

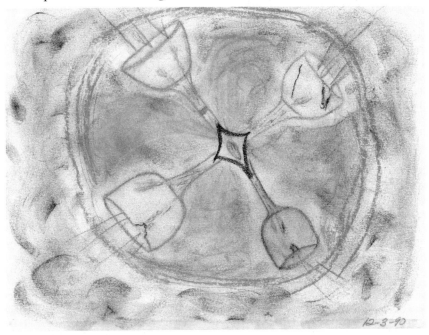

As integration began we experienced a swirling blur of color, as if someone had dropped different colors of paint onto a potter's wheel that was spinning ever faster to blend the colors. As the colors swirled and blended, we experienced sadness, joy, and strength. All of our gifts and resources were available and united. We became aware that we would no longer operate separately—something we had always prided ourselves on being able to do. We were no longer alone; we were the one whole person we dreamed of and were created to be. We felt as if we were coming home, and we shared the joy of homecoming as well as the tears of grief as we accepted how much we had lost. Permeable boundaries were installed, allowing complete access to thoughts, emotions, and skills; the desire to be together; and total acceptance. There were—and still are—no words to describe the awe we felt experiencing all the detached emotions and senses.

The Holy Spirit kept me in this place and state for a little while, letting me relish it and solidify myself in it. After a time It told me it was time to move on with the session. David returned his attention to the outline, and slowly I returned to the awareness of others in the room.

Journey's End I attained completeness as one person in awareness and skills. It was completely new and unfamiliar.

Immediately after integration came a period of ecstasy. Colors were brighter, sounds were clearer and softer. The body— our body, my body—seemed to move more slowly and feel more relaxed. I was surprised by the fact that I could feel my skin, that my skin had texture and the texture varied over my body. I found I had clear vision, not the double or triple vision I had previously experienced. I did not have to struggle to focus when I first opened my eyes, the way I'd had to in previous sessions. I saw things up close, not as if I were in a faraway world or in a dream state. I felt energized and fatigued at the same time. The work I had just done, my integration, was both exhilarating and exhausting. I felt clear-headed. I was shocked by the silence in my head; the silence felt wonderful, but now I was alone. I was free.

David concluded the session by debriefing everyone in the room. The others offered feedback about what they had witnessed and how the session had affected them. They asked me what was the same and what was immediately different between being integrated and being split up. Their questions helped me stabilize myself in the newness of integration: What was my vision like? What about my hearing, what was it like? What was I experiencing in my head? What was I thinking about? How did my body feel? I answered their questions the best I could. It was hard since I was searching for words to describe what was so new.

Without Mary and the Holy Spirit, none of us would have been strong enough to see this journey through. I understood the journey was not over; I had to solidify new and healthy coping skills. The Holy Spirit assured me It would continue to be with me and help me.

Post Integration

After we achieved full integration and remained one, I reflected on how all the temporary integration's had actually increased the system's desire to work together, because the alters could see what integration provided. This helped me recognize those brief periods of wholeness as positive steps forward instead of failures and steps backward.

The first thing I noticed days after integration was the distortion of time. I seemed to have more of it. I completed projects in less time than before, so I could do more. It seemed as if I had twice the time I'd had before integration. I didn't feel quite so tired. Because time seemed longer, I found I was unable to cook. Everything I prepared came out undercooked, but when I tried to compensate, I burned it. I misjudged travel time when heading for appointments, arriving 30-45 minutes early.

My coordination when knitting and sewing was poor. I became depressed over what I perceived I had lost. I seemed unable to adjust. I began thinking I should have remained split up. David and I discussed this, taking it to the Holy Spirit. I received silence from my spiritual support. I began to realize that how I contacted the Holy Spirit had also changed. Before integration I could easily move into a deeply meditative state during my talks with the Holy Spirit. Before integration meditation has been something I never thought about. It just happened like my switching just happened. All my life I had talked to and depended on the Holy Spirit to survive. I talked to the Holy Spirit throughout the day like I might talk to any person I ran into. Now I had to learn how to allow myself to be free for the Holy Spirit to take me where It wanted me. Now I had to learn to consciously let myself be free. I had to learn how to allow the Holy Spirit to move me into the meditative state, I couldn't move myself there. I did this by asking the Holy Spirit to show me how I had in various alter states learned to trust It before.

The Holy Spirit answered my request by allowing me to review how the alters and I had allowed ourselves to be free before integration. I studied it much the same way Erik Erickson, who was crippled by polio, studied how his body had moved when he was able to walk. He concentrated on moving the muscles just the right way so that he could move his legs again. (He went from using a wheelchair to being able to walk again). I also used the tapes of my sessions to help me learn. Watching the tapes brought back the memory of the experience so I could learn what to recognize. Once I returned to my restful place of meditation, I recognized how the Holy Spirit had been helping me. It clearly told me to give myself time. I understood I needed to make many adjustments before life would seem to function with order again. The Holy Spirit was right; my adjustments have tested my patience.

At 11 months post integration I thought I had split into the various alters again. This was caused by my reaction to a homily I heard in church. The homily was on anger and the priest said that if we were angry than we had already committed murder in our heart. When I was growing up I heard this homily regularly as well as hearing I had no right to be angry. In fact if my brothers or I displayed any anger at all we were beaten.

Throughout my childhood the Third Commandment had been "drummed" into my brothers and me; "Honor thy father and mother". We were forcefully reminded this meant obedience. In my childhood obedience meant accepting the abuse and then being told it was for our own good, to shut up-it didn't hurt, that what was being done to us was for knowledge for when we were married, or that we caused what we were getting. It was the same presentation that had been used to help justify abuse more than 30 years earlier. I used some of the skills David and Lee taught me. I confronted the Priest on his misinterpretation of the scripture reading. I said that the reading referred to our behavior resulting from anger and what we did with the anger. Then I referenced Christ's anger cited in the scriptures.

After reflecting and searching I found my integration was intact. What I had thought was a splitting-apart was actually my moving through the permeable boundaries, experiencing all the emotions and resources needed to be able to cope with the particular situation. I needed the anger I had been denied more than 30 years ago to confront the teaching that was, and often still is, used to justify abuse. Now, when an event (whether positive or negative) triggers a memory, I remain my whole self, an adult, feeling the emotions and sensations necessary to bring closure to past memories and coping skills while strengthening my newer, more mature skills.

Fourteen months post integration found me with restored cooking and knitting skills as well as improved coordination. I was less hyper-vigilant (over aware of my environment). I became less vigilant of my environment and more aware of myself. As the months after integration passed, I continued to be amazed at how long a day was, at how I accomplished in one day what I remembered having done in two days (until I worked on this book; then I really slowed down). I understood more of what I read. I remembered conversations. My writing was consistent, and I no longer felt as if something was wrong with me. I learned to recognize the warning signs when I was or am at risk of splitting (dissociating). Change and growth continued.

At 32 months post integration I attended a retreat. I really didn't expect anything from this retreat. I just needed a rest. What I received was a gift of healing. The retreat started on a Wednesday and during that first night on retreat I was awakened at 3 a.m. I was unable to get back to sleep so I prayed. During prayer I had a vision that left me confused.

In the first vision I was wearing a fleece cape printed with geometric shapes that suggested a Southwest Indian design. I was standing in a clearing in the mountains where trees were being stacked for milling. God told me to pray for the trees, the clearing, and the sawmill.

Thursday the second night of the retreat I was again woke up about 3 a.m. In the second vision I was still wearing the cape. God led me to a mountain peak. I looked across the mountain to another ridge and saw someone asleep on a yellow mat on the edge of a ledge. The mat started sliding off the ledge. I reached out to try to stop the person from falling, but God pulled my arm back, saying, "No, this must be." I saw the person fall off the ledge, and the vision ended.

I had a third vision occur on the third night of the retreat which was a Friday. I was wearing a white cape. Again God took me to the top of a mountain. He placed me on a white platform balanced carefully on the edge of the mountain ridge. I looked out over the world and saw a river flowing thousands of feet below me. God asked me if I would serve him. Although I heard God say the word "serve," I saw the word "surrender" written across the sky. I hesitated, but then said yes. God told me to prostrate myself before Him, and when I did I fell off the mountain. I saw myself plummeting toward the ground and closed my eyes, yet I felt no fear. A sudden gust of wind caught me in the chest and knocked the breath out of me. I was physically awake and aware that I was having a vision. I gasped in response to the impact, then I felt myself rise. In the vision I opened my eyes and discovered I was rising and falling at the same instant. I looked around and realized I was plummeting into the depths of Christ. I could see creases, crevices, and secret places. The vision ended.

I carried a cape to the retreat to wear outside. It was a reversible cape: one side was an Indian print, the other side was white. I had been wearing the Indian print side out but on Saturday I reversed it so the white side was out when I wore it. During the evening services I prostrated myself before God, surrendering my will to His will. I forgot about the visions. I prayed and then I sat up. Everything seemed fine. Nothing special happened until someone walked up behind me and placed a hand on my head to pray with me. I collapsed into a prone position. I struggled with an intense headache, and someone prayed for my freedom from the headache. God brought me a memory that needed emotional healing. He held me in His arms while He helped me grieve and let go of my terror from the physical violence I was remembering from my childhood. He brought a particular type of healing; emotional healing, to an area of my life that I had no idea needed healing. After this experience I realized the visions had been preparation for the healing God planned for me. I also realized that I was wearing my cape with the white side out. And I understood more of what God had been trying to tell me in the visions.

What I understood in the visions was that God was using past experiences I could identify with to prepare me for healing. God asked me in the first vision to pray in the woods. In hindsight, the symbolism of praying for the trees was important because when I was a child I use to run and hide in the woods. The woods protected me. When I felt afraid or in danger, I poured out my fears to God in the woods (I prayed to God in the woods). In the vision the trees were being cleared out and milled into lumber for building projects or furniture. The symbolism for me in the trees being cleared and milled was that God was taking my poured out pain and turning it into something positive for my present and future.

I am now more than five years post integration, and I continue to receive special moments of healing from God. Recently I fell and broke my wrist. After setting the wrist the doctor had to saw a split in the cast to allow for swelling. When I heard the saw I recalled another memory, this one more than 40 years old. As a child I had to spend the years between ages 1 and 4 in body casts or leg casts from the waist down. I became terrified each time a doctor cut into one of those casts, because I didn't understand that the saw wasn't going to cut me too. The doctor and my parents would get frustrated with me and my fear and yell at me to stop my crying or screaming, that the saw was not going to hurt me. Now, some 40 years later, I received healing for the terror I'd experienced as a little girl—terror adults did not understand or know how to dispel. (A side note on my broken wrist, when the doctor cut the cast off, the saw pushed cast material into my flesh cutting my wrist).

...Each time God offers to heal me I have to embrace the wound and hold it out to Him for His style of first aid. Experience has taught me that God's first aid is restorative, while my first aid usually causes infections. God cleans the full depth of

the wound; I stay on the surface to avoid pain. Healing will never end for me, and it shouldn't. Healing is not necessarily easy, and that is okay because after each healing episode I am less and less afraid of the pain. Because of this I am more willing to embrace the uncertainty of God's ways so I can have His gift of restoration and wholeness, something every human needs. I find a particular truth in one verse from the poem "Deep Within": "Retrieving un-retrievable memories will be a lifelong process ending too soon" I believe we all die before we retrieve everything we need to heal from.

NOTES

NOTES

Chapter Six
Reflection

When I began therapy with David, Mary was the first one I allowed to help me overcome my fear of revealing my past. When I asked her to help me, she drew me to water. She encouraged me to join her in the ocean, where she held us while we cried, our tears mixing with the waves that rolled in.

Later, after I had told David of my talks with the Holy Spirit, he invited me to bring the Holy Spirit into therapy. The Holy Spirit came regularly, accompanied by Mary. They offered me gentleness and support. We were not used to such gentleness and kindness; it had been years since we had last recognized their care for us. When I began to once again feel their acceptance, I felt as if I were crumpling into a ball. I felt as if a dam had ruptured inside of me. I became lost in my emotions as Mary and the Holy Spirit gave permission for me to feel.

We began telling Mary our fears and shame. She showed us a path leading to our previous safe place that had been a physical place from my childhood but was now a mental place for me as an adult, and she invited us to accompany her. We followed her, climbing ever higher and deeper into the mountains. We were afraid someone could see us so high up, but Mary showed us that the path was hidden from "prying eyes." A protector had been positioned to guard the safe place and prepare it for each of us as we arrived. Once I overcame the fear of being seen, I willingly ascended to safety and did not want to leave.

It was important for me and for each alter to investigate our safe place as well as the external surroundings. This was necessary if we were to begin trusting one another. It was necessary so that we would develop the desire to be truly free in spirit.

Mary, Jesus, and the Holy Spirit were the only ones who were able to help us find the courage to venture and explore. David would regularly remind us to listen and follow the Holy Spirit's and Mary's directions between sessions, to ask them if it was okay, if it was safe, to leave the safe place. When one of us became fearful and unwilling to explore or to go further, David called that alter back to Mary and the Holy Spirit, asking what we needed. He asked which was better: to stay where we were or to go with Mary and the Holy Spirit. Exploring our surroundings and the safe place meant that each of us could learn of our life, of the things we had endured and the feelings we had in a safe, non-threatening way. And if we needed to rest and heal, the safe place would be our refuge.

The journey through the safe place was difficult. The exploration began in the complete darkness each of us cherished, with David facilitating the journey. The Holy Spirit guided us in and out of crevices and holes, first peeking at our secrets, then helping us develop the strength we needed until we were strong enough to take and hold the experiences ourselves.

The Holy Spirit and Mary worked with each aspect separately, drawing them out from behind rocks, coaxing some out of the caves and tunnels they were hiding in, always allowing them the freedom to retreat when any experience was overwhelming. Eventually each part was able to freely move in and out of the safe place alone.

The next challenge was to begin introducing them to one another much the way a handler might introduce a guard dog to each visitor: one at a time, always studying the dog's behavior so as not to over-stimulate the animal and provoke an attack. For me, this approach was necessary since a couple of alters were protective, guarding others and their secrets. They were willing to die or suffer injury as well as injure others to fulfill their responsibilities.

Slowly we made our way through each part of our journey, exploring one another and our experiences. The safe place brightened as it began moving toward a brilliant light that was at once warm and cool, scary and exciting, sad and joyous. As Mary and the Holy Spirit entered this light, they encouraged hesitant alters to join them and other alters who were already in the light. They had to encourage them much the same way a parent needs to encourage a child to enter the classroom the first day of kindergarten. Some of us preferred to stay on the periphery of the light while others totally fled. The Holy Spirit moved in and out of the light, drawing in all who hesitated. Mary stayed in the light with those of us who chose to stay with her. Mary's presence provided the same sense of security that the presence of most parents would provide for a child in a strange place. The Holy Spirit and Mary were always with us, offering peace to our troubled spirits. Each of us found we had the freedom to leave the presence of the Holy Spirit and Mary, which we often did until we allowed ourselves to experience, desire, and accept the peace waiting for us. David facilitated the alters' decisions to allow themselves this peace, and as they did so, they found complete acceptance. Once the peace and acceptance were shared, none wanted to give it up and return to being alone in the dark.

The voice of the Holy Spirit was strong, firm, and gentle. It never commanded me to do or say anything; It simply spoke, challenging and inviting. We were comfortable and familiar enough with the Holy Spirit that we would lose track of all else when we were with It. Because the Holy Spirit never demanded anything of us, we felt secure with our arguments against working together, listening, and revealing our past (which we thought justified our resistance). During these times David would interject critical questions such as, "You can't or you won't?" "Is the Guidance (his word for the Holy Spirit) or Mary silent, or you won't listen?" and "Have you moved away from them and now cannot hear them?" When he did this it was like drawing the point of a pin along a nerve, eliciting a response that always challenged the logic we used. While David challenged our logic and beliefs, the Holy Spirit waited patiently for us to catch up and join it, much the way a parent waits for a child who is squatting on the beach, picking at a shell in the sand.

When times of terror, intense fear, or feelings of danger occurred, we would curl up with Jesus, the Holy Spirit, or Mary and allow them to encapsulate us in protection. This encapsulation felt like I was sitting in someone's lap with the person's arms around me, rocking me, warming me. Other times it felt like a warm blanket encasing me, as in a cocoon. Protected like this, we could rest or sleep. During these restful times, Mary and the Holy Spirit reassured us, helping us correct the thoughts and beliefs we had grown up with.

When my alter system invited the Holy Spirit and Mary to help us in our journey, we received not only their help but also their deep commitment to loyalty and friendship. Several things occurred to demonstrate this.

- Sometimes we refused to tell David what the Holy Spirit suggested because we either thought the idea was ridiculous or we just didn't want to do it. When we resisted, the Holy Spirit would tell us to "follow David's lead, he knows what to do." This was all I would tell David. It turned out that what David suggested would be exactly what the Holy Spirit told us. Sometimes we felt stupid and other times we felt angered by this.
- The Holy Spirit and Mary were firm foundations that kept us from being swept away by the current of our mental and emotional storms.
- Jesus, Mary, and the Holy Spirit held fast to us when we felt too exhausted to hold on anymore.
- The Holy Spirit instructed David about what needed to happen next, whether we were ready to move on or needed to continue what we were doing.
- Jesus, Mary, and the Holy Spirit did not abandon us when some of us told them to get out of our lives.
- The Holy Spirit and Jesus provided the male strengths I needed for recovery when it would have been inappropriate for David to do so, and Mary provided the female strengths when Lee couldn't.

The Holy Spirit and Mary showed us bits and pieces of our life, pointing out the role modeling provided by my grandma, her twin sister, and animals leading us to where we were soon to be: ready for integration, ready to be the whole person we never felt we were, to have our memories and not think we were insane. The Holy Spirit assured us we were correct when we sensed the time was coming to close the past. Our memories were not haunting us as much, and we could finally begin to move into the present and future.

Where am I today? I cannot watch violent movies such as "The Prince of Tides." Doing so causes my emotions to wash over me like a torrential downpour as I remember the fear, terror, loneliness, intimidation, and control my siblings and I lived through. I will not allow myself to live in an isolated area the way my family did during my childhood.

Are things different for me after integration? Yes. Today I am aware of more good than bad in my life. I am no longer self-injurious. I no longer force my body to work beyond its physical capacity. My pain has lessened, although I feel pain more quickly and more intensely than I used to. An example of this is surgery I had in December 1997. I underwent surgery to correct a problem in my nose so I could breathe without difficulty. I did not expect too much post-operative pain since I had never suffered much pain from any other surgical procedure. I was unprepared for this pain. I guess I was fully aware of it and able to feel it because I was not sharing it among several alters. I was whole and feeling all the pain myself.

Now I feel the touch as well as the temperature of water on my skin. I used to wash in water hotter than 120 degrees and not feel its heat. I knew the water had been hot only because my skin turned red. Now if I run water hotter than 110 degrees, I have to cool it down before I can use it.

My health has improved, marked by a significant decrease in allergic reactions and fewer infections. My skin looks more evenly colored and clearer to me. People who have known me for five years or longer tell me I look more rested and have better color. My sleep patterns are more consistent, and void of shadows and conversations. I usually remember what I study and read. My positive self-concept is evident to me; I don't constantly second-guess myself. People tell me I have an "air of confidence," an "air of assurance" about me and time continues to be long.

It is easier for me to recognize truth for what it is and face it head on than to turn away from it. My startle response has decreased from lasting four to five hours to lasting only five minutes. I laugh and cry freely. I now recognize my emotions as genuine; they are no longer stoic or trapped behind a brick wall. My body's memories no longer carry the extreme pain and behavior they once did. I like being female, with all its gifts.

Are things the same after integration? Yes. I still live with pain. X rays still show the same damage located in the same places. I still balance gentleness with firmness in my life. Whereas alters previously existed and worked separately from one another, they now are one and work together. I still have the skills and abilities I had before integration, and I still have a wide range of interests. I paint, write, and create whenever I feel danger or rage. In the past I was never able to destroy anything, even when I felt like smashing something. I still cannot bring myself to destroy anything; I saw too much of that in my life.

Healing continues. Moving to Alaska has provided opportunities for healing where I did not know I needed healing. I was raised in the North and moving to Alaska brought me home to face spiritual healing. Attending church up north brought back memories of how scriptures were interpreted by the pastor and then re-interpreted by those of us listening to the sermons. The interpretations were used in my family to justify the abuse we lived with. We were taught that anger is a sin, that if we get angry we have already committed murder in our hearts (children were not allowed to be angry). We were also told that children always obey their parents, no matter what the parents say or do. While these may be good beliefs they need to be clarified and interpreted correctly. Too many times people take things literally and out of context.

Moving to Alaska has also allowed good memories to surface, reminding me of the good times in my childhood. Among my happiest memories are foraging for berries and other wild food, building snowmen and snow forts, and ice-skating.

I find myself looking forward to the next 35 years and the aging process, excited about the changes I will go through. I feel as if I have been given a second chance to live and to be aware of life; I don't want to lose it. I am more aware of what is happening in the world around me. I am able to laugh and cry more freely. God has blessed me. I am grateful for the opportunity to be an integrated person. I will continue to remain in contact with the Holy Spirit, who along with Mary is ever present to share my joys and sorrows.

Sometimes post integration causes me to be sad, because certain events remind me of what I have missed, such as attending a prom. Sometimes I am reminded of having survived a personal war that left scars invisible to the rest of the world. I still have no memory of much of my life. As time passes I know I will be granted more memories. I also know there is much I may never retrieve, and that is difficult for me to accept because I want it all.

I end this book with three thoughts on the role of spirituality in any healing journey, clarification of a statement I made at the beginning of this book, and one final poem. Here are my three thoughts on the role of spirituality in a healing journey:

- Getting in touch with our spirituality is meant to help us heal. It is not to be used to run away and escape experiences in life. It is a part of who we are, helping us know where we came from and where we are going. It is given by God to provide us strength for life.
- Spirituality requires action on our part. God is always with us when we accept Him in our lives, but He seldom provides a "quick fix" to the pain of this world. Every one of us needs to work hand-in-hand with God.
- The person I am called by God to be, the person I was created to be, was always within me. I had to look back to see where I came from before I could look ahead to see where I was going. I had to know my past to be free to enjoy my future.

When I began this book I referred to the fact that I was one whole rather than many parts. It is vital to remember that people living through abuse do not need pity or sympathy. We need healing, understanding, empathy, and uncompromising love. I believe these thoughts adequately sum up the life and healing experience of everyone, not just those of us diagnosed with DID.

In the introduction I made a statement that may have surprised you. I wrote that my parents were the best parents for me, that had I had different parents I would not be half the person I am today. This comment is true! Because I had the parents I had, I learned several valuable lessons. I learned not to lie. Amid their prejudice I learned to be open-minded. They taught me to try and to keep trying until I succeeded. They taught me to seek truth and not to quit until I found it. My parents taught me to think and behave critically, not to simply "follow the crowd." Finally, they taught me not to be afraid of work or of hard work. These qualities helped me enter therapy and see it through to completion.

The lies of my life drove me to find truth. My constant drive to sacrifice my own emotional state to preserve others' taught me to stop and to be aware of how I judge myself and others, and how to begin to love, especially myself. I returned time and again to heal my wounds, in spite of the pain. This was hard work, harder than any strenuous manual labor I ever did. I am truly grateful for my parents, and I thank God for them. As I look back over this entire journey, I realize God did not lead me into counseling, He led me into what is known as deep healing. Only deep healing truly cleanses our heart and mind and restores life.

TODAY

The day begins quiet as all within sleep.
One by one we begin rising to start our routine.
We move about in such a way so as not to disturb any others.
We move on light feet trying to keep all this stillness within, but
soon the peace is disturbed as others begin to wake.
The day begins as each waking person goes about their tasks
interfering with no other.
Now, here we stand ready to once again face a day
but this day is different as is every day.
Today we will listen and feel, we will love and challenge.
We will again step out of ourself, this time to see how we do.
Will we meet the challenge of another day and survive
or will we be too weak to go on and die.
Each day finds that we do both, We live and we die.

NOTES

NOTES

References

Bilich, M., & Carlson, S. (1994). Therapists and clergy working together: Linking the psychological with the spiritual in the treatment of MPD. The Journal of Christian Healing. 16 (1), 3-11.

Bryant, D., Keesler, J., & Shirar, L. (1992). The family inside: Working with the multiple. New York: W.W. Norton & Company. Clark, T., & Arterburn, S. (1993). More than one. Nashville: Oliver Nelson Books.

Comstock, C. (1985, October). Internal self helpers or centers. Paper presented at the Second International Congress on Multiple Personalities and Dissociative States, Chicago. IL.

Cornell, W. F. & Olio, K. A. (1991). Integrating affect in treatment with adult survivors of physical and sexual abuse. American Journal of Orthopsychiatry, 61(1), 59-69.

Fine, C. G. (1991). Treatment stabilization and crises prevention: Pacing the treatment of the multiple personality disorder patient. Psychiatric Clinics of North America, 14 (3), 661-675.

Friesen, J. G. (1991). Uncovering the mystery of MPD. San Bernardino: Here's Life Publishers. Hicks, R. (1993). Failure to Scream. Nashville: Oliver Nelson Books.

Kraft, C. H. (1993). Deep wounds, deep healing. Ann Arbor: Servant Publications Kluft, R. P. (1991). Clinical presentation of multiple personality disorder. Psychiatric Clinic of North America, 14 (3), 605-629.

Kluft, R. P. (1991). Hospital treatment of multiple personality disorder. Psychiatric Clinics of North America, 14 (3), 695-719.

Marmer, S. S. (1991). Multiple personality disorder. Psychiatric Clinics of North America, 14 (3), 677-693.

Panos, P. T., Panos,A. & Allred, G. H. (1990). The need for marriage therapy in the treatment of multiple personality disorder. Dissociation, 13 (1), 10-13.

Posttraumatic therapy. In J. P. Wilson & B. Raphael (Eds.),International handbook of Traumatic Stress Syndromes (pp.773-783). New York: Plenum Press.

Putnam, F. W. (1989). Diagnosis & treatment of multiple personality disorder. New York: Guilford Press.

Putnam, F. W. (1991). Dissociative disorders in children and adolescents: A developmental perspective. Psychiatric Clinic of North America, 14 (3), 519-531.

Putnam, F. W. (1991). Recent research on multiple personality disorder. Psychiatric Clinics of North America, 14 (3), 489-502.

Sachs, R. G., Frischholz, E. J., & Wood, J. I. (1988). Marital and family therapy in the treatment of multiple personality disorder. Journal of Marital and Marital Family Therapy, 14 (3), 249-259.

Spiegel, D., & Cardens, E. (1991). Disintegrated experience: The dissociative disorder revisited. Journal of Abnormal Psychology, 100 (3), 366-378.

Turkus, J. A. (1991). Psychotherapy and case management for multiple personality disorder: Synthesis for continuity of care. Psychiatric Clinics of North America, 14 (3), 649-660.